CLEANING MADE EASY

ARTIFICIAL FLOWERS: Place silk flowers head down in a large paper bag containing ordinary table salt. Shake vigorously.

BOOKS: To remove a grease spot, put a paper towel on either side of the page and press gently with a warm iron.

CANDLESTICKS: Pour warm water into the candle holder to soften the old wax, then remove wax from the outer surface by pushing it off gently with a soft cloth wrapped around your finger. *Do not scrape dried wax off with a knife.*

PLUS: Diamond Rings . . . Embroidery . . . Floor Tiles . . . Glassware . . . Hairbrushes . . . Ironing Board Covers . . . Jade . . . Kitchen Cabinets . . . Linen . . . Music Boxes . . . Oil Paintings . . . Pianos . . . Rattan . . . Silk . . . Terrazzo . . . Upholstery . . . Venetian Blinds . . . Wallpaper . . . **AND MUCH, MUCH MORE!**

HOW TO CLEAN ABSOLUTELY EVERYTHING

Barty Phillips

AVON BOOKS ◆ NEW YORK

Modern materials are complex in their make-up and so are the substances which cause dirt and stains. Modern chemicals, too, are diverse and can be dangerous. Keep them out of reach of children and use them with caution and according to the manufacturer's instructions (see also "A-Z of Household Products" on page 164). When cleaning any item, test the cleaning agent on a small, undetectable part of the surface first to see what result you get and, if in doubt, take it to a professional right away, particularly if it is antique or valuable. The publisher and author will not be held responsible for any damage or loss which may occur from following the procedures in this book.

HOW TO CLEAN ABSOLUTELY EVERYTHING was originally published in the United Kingdom, but has never before appeared in book form in the United States.

AVON BOOKS
A division of
The Hearst Corporation
1350 Avenue of the Americas
New York, New York 10019

Copyright © 1990, 1995 by Barty Phillips
Published by arrangement with the author
Library of Congress Catalog Card Number: 94-96285
ISBN: 0-380-77736-3

First Avon Books Printing: April 1995

AVON TRADEMARK REG. U.S. PAT. OFF. AND IN OTHER COUNTRIES, MARCA REGISTRADA, HECHO EN U.S.A.

Printed in the U.S.A.

RA 10 9 8 7 6 5 4 3 2 1

Contents

Introduction

I clean, you clean, we all clean. In the last half century we
have been aided and abetted by innumerable household
chemicals to make things brighter, whiter, shinier, and more
hygienic with less effort.

Unfortunately, such thoroughness is often not good for the
environment and not good for us. Caustics burn, phosphates
pollute, perfumes and enzymes cause skin problems, most
household chemicals are highly poisonous. And the worst of
it is that we don't know what we are using half the time because there is no law that says labels have to carry a list of
ingredients, as they do in food products.

This book does not dismiss chemical and proprietary cleaners out of hand—they have their uses in certain situations—
but it does offer alternatives for those who prefer not to be
polluting the environment or damaging their bodies. Both
man-made and natural fibers require fairly specialized knowledge, but once you know what is needed they are not difficult
to clean effectively and, indeed, are often cleaned more easily
with natural products than with chemicals.

Where appropriate this book offers three ways of cleaning:

1. The "right" way, which is the most painstaking and thorough way, tried, tested, and recommended by the experts
   but by no means necessarily the best way for everyday
   cleaning.

2. The "lazy" way, which chooses shortcuts where these
   make sense. Don't think that lazy is a derogatory term

1

here. On the contrary, anyone who can find ways of doing a satisfactory cleaning job using less effort or time merits a bonus mark for initiative.

3. The third way is the "green" way or the environmentally friendly way. It is not always easy to define "green." Is it greener to put trash in plastic bags or paper bags? Plastic is not considered to be a green material and usually it is not biodegradable. But the making of paper uses a precious (if renewable) natural resource.

And do you believe the manufacturers who tell you their laundry detergent is green because it contains no nitrates? You shouldn't because nitrates are not an ingredient of laundry detergents anyway. What we'd like to know is what IS in the product, not what isn't.

The green answer to cleaning is that it is fairly safe to use less of any cleaning agent than the manufacturers recommend and to try to stick to natural (which often means edible) cleaning agents such as vinegar, lemon juice, and baking soda. At least then you will be doing less damage. Happily the green way is often the lazy way as well, so you can combine the two with a good conscience.

Employing a cleaner

The ultimate lazy way for any type of cleaning is to hire someone else to do it, whether it's a carpet cleaner, a window cleaner, or someone to come in and help with the housework. The lazy alternatives given in this book are for people who simply don't have the time for anything else. Hiring a cleaner may be the answer if you don't have the time even for the "lazy way."

- When choosing a cleaner make sure you find somebody who comes with personal recommendations and who is good at the type of work you want done. There is no point in hiring a full-time housekeeper if all you want is the bathroom cleaned thoroughly.

- Always, and particularly if you are hiring someone permanent, treat them well. Pay them the going rate for the area, no less and no more. Don't leave unnecessary chaos for them to cope with and then complain because you can't find things. If you find somebody you want and they have to (and are prepared to) travel some distance to get to you, pay a little extra to cover the fare.

- Don't give anyone your front door key unless or until you know them and have confidence in them.

- It's useful if you can be at home when they arrive or before they leave so that you build up a personal relationship. You'll get a more caring service that way.

- Don't feel forced to hire somebody twice a week or even once a week if all you want is a thorough going over once every two weeks.

- Make sure you both understand precisely what you want done. There are such things as "treasures" who can read your mind and will do all tasks unbidden, but they are few and far between. You may find it helpful to refer your cleaner to this book.

- A useful alternative to hiring somebody permanently is to get a cleaning company to "blitzclean" the house for a fairly steep sum, but then you won't be getting it done that often. Look in the Yellow Pages. Some cleaners only deal with contract cleaning jobs, others will cover domestic cleaning.

This book is intended to be an easy and quick reference guide whether you are dealing with everyday objects, something precious, something not encountered before, or even an emergency. I hope most everyday cleaning situations are covered here and that you will find the solutions effective.

Throughout the text "soap" refers to true soap and "detergent" refers to synthetic detergents. The various A-Z sections will tell you how to deal with specific materials, specific stains, and specific objects around the home. There is also a guide to cleaning products.

I hope you will enjoy using this book and treat it like a friend.

Laundering

Doing the laundry is one of those thankless tasks that just has to be done. But with modern machines to wash and dry the laundry for you, there's no excuse for feeling a sense of martyrdom about it.

It isn't quite as simple as throwing everything dirty that you can lay your hands on into the machine and pressing the start button, however. Do this and you could open the washing machine at the end of its cycle to discover that your white tablecloth now matches your new crimson sweater, which has itself shrunk beyond recognition.

THE CARE LABELS

Modern fabrics can be made of innumerable different yarns ranging from natural fibers like wool, cotton, linen, and silk to man-made ones like rayon, acetate, nylon, polyester, and so on, or mixtures of any of these. Each material has special requirements of its own and the only way to be certain of getting a good wash without damaging a garment is to follow the instructions on its care label. Most garments produced nowadays have such a label, which tells you if an item is washable and, if so, how it should be washed (i.e. at what temperature). They also indicate if fabrics should be dry-cleaned only.

Preparing the clothes

Whether washing by hand or machine, first prepare the items as follows.

• Do up zips and buttons, hooks and eyes, and snaps that may cause damage to other items in the wash.

• Sew on loose or missing buttons and mend any small tears.

• Remove debris from pockets.

• Brush off any loose dirt, especially dried mud. Dog and cat hairs can be removed with masking tape: Press a strip on to the garment and pull it off—the hairs should come off with it. Or buy a fur-removal roller at your local pet store.

• Tie up any ribbons, strings, sashes, etc.

• If you are a loser of socks, use socks clips (available from drugstores) to hold each pair together.

Sorting the clothes

Sort all items into groups of the same color and with the same instructions. If a garment has no care label (secondhand garments may pre-date the labeling regulations), wash it in a cool, gentle wash cycle in the machine or wash it by hand. Alternatively have it dry-cleaned.

Testing for colorfastness

Test new items for colorfastness before washing with other colors. Test a hidden area of the garment such as under the arm or at the back of the hem.

1. Dampen a cotton ball or tissue and leave it on the fabric for five minutes.

2. If any dye comes off on the cotton ball or tissue, wash the garment separately or have it dry-cleaned.

3. If the color has not run, it can be washed with white articles or other colors, provided you don't use the hottest water.

Pre-wash treatments to loosen dirt

Removing stains

Look over each garment carefully and treat for stains if necessary. There are various products on the market that will loosen most stains before washing. You can use a spray or stain removal soap that you rub on the mark. Use it on collars and cuffs and for stains such as make-up, sauce, wine, wax polishes, hair spray, medicines, egg, coffee, beet juice, suntan lotion, etc. Or rub heavily with chalk, which will absorb the oils, and once the oil is removed the dirt will come off easily. See Chapter 3 for how to tackle specific stains.

Pre-washing

Very grubby work clothes, and other heavily-soiled garments should be given a pre-wash in the washing machine.

Soaking

A very effective pre-wash treatment is to soak clothes in detergent and water before washing. It's not necessary to use strong detergent—it's the soaking that gets the dirt out.

- For obstinate stains rub detergent in before soaking.
- Make sure the detergent is thoroughly dissolved before putting the clothes in, or use liquid detergent.
- Don't soak colors and whites together.
- Don't soak silk, wool, leather, flame-retardant fabrics, non-colorfast fabrics or drip-dry fabrics.

Bleaching

Bleaching is a pre-wash treatment for removing stubborn stains from white fabrics (but see page 38). Liquid household bleaches are usually based on chlorine and they remove stains by adding oxygen. They should not be used on silk or wool.

Sodium perborate (one of the main ingredients of "colorsafe" non-chlorine bleaches, like Clorox 2) is also an oxidizing bleach. Sodium perborate bleaches are safe to use on silk and wool.

- To bleach a whole article in chlorine bleach use 2 teaspoons of bleach to 2½ gallons of cold water. Immerse the article for 10 to 15 minutes. Rinse thoroughly before washing as usual.

- Never use undiluted chlorine bleach.

- Never use chlorine bleach on silk, wool, rayon, drip-dry cottons, or any article with a stain-resistant finish. Follow the manufacturer's instructions when using chlorine bleach.

- A milder bleach is hydrogen peroxide (available from drugstores), which can be used on silk and wool. Use in a solution of 1 part hydrogen peroxide to 8 parts water. Items can be soaked for up to 12 hours unless made of silk or wool, which should never be soaked. Rinse thoroughly before washing as usual. (See also page 39.)

MACHINE WASHING—THE RIGHT WAY

- Load the machine correctly. Overloading will prevent the clothes from moving around freely, and they will not get clean.

- Select the correct cycle.

- Don't use too much detergent—slightly less than the manufacturer's recommended amount should be sufficient. If you think there's some detergent left in the clothes after rinsing, put them through an extra rinse cycle. Leftover detergent in the fabric will attract dirt.

- Add fabric softener to the dispenser if desired (see below).
- Prevent colored dyes from running by putting salt in the wash or in the soaking water.
- Man-made fabrics need to be rinsed in cold water so that creases don't set. See that you choose a suitable cycle.
- After a color wash or after bleaching in the washing machine, put the machine through a rinse cycle so that the next load does not pick up any dye or bleach.
- After each wash, unplug the washing machine and wipe it down both inside and out using a clean, damp cloth to remove any last traces of chlorine or bleach.

Fabric softeners

These can be added to the final rinse, whether machine or hand washing, to leave fabrics softer to the touch. Follow the manufacturer's instructions.

- They are particularly good for babies' clothes and diapers, sweaters, towels, and other soft garments worn or used next to the skin.
- They make ironing easier and prevent the static electricity that can occur with nylon and other man-made materials.

Drying

- Don't overload the dryer, and do take the clothes out as soon as the machine has stopped.
- Don't tumble-dry acrylics at a high setting.
- Never tumble-dry wool.
- Fold clothes (if completely dry) the moment you take them from the dryer—they should need little or no ironing.
- Tumble-drying sometimes causes static, which can make

clothes cling to the body. Ten minutes of cold tumble at the end of the drying cycle can reduce this effect. Or you can add a sheet of fabric softener (like Cling Free) to the dryer.

- If you can hang your clothes on an outside line instead of putting them in the dryer they will smell fresh, have a soft texture, and if the sun is out, it will help to bleach them.

Machine washing—the lazy way

- If you have no time for mending tears and securing loose buttons before washing, put garments loosely in a pillow case so they don't tear further in the wash.

- Use a short, cool wash cycle for whites and "fast" colored garments together—unless the care label specifically warns to wash a garment separately.

- If you have no time to wash tights and pantyhose by hand, collect them up and wash them together in a loosely knotted pillow case, so they don't get tangled up.

- Leave out the soaking, bleaching, etc., stage.

Machine washing—the green way

- Whenever possible use low temperature washes, economy washes, and half-load cycles, to save water and electricity.

- Don't use the washing machine if you only have two or three items—wash them by hand instead or wait until you have a full load.

- Use an environmentally "friendly" detergent.

- Most fabric softeners have added perfumes to which many people are allergic. You can create your own fabric softener by using a water softener in the rinse or even a water softener and half the normal amount of detergent in the wash. Or use a non-perfumed hair conditioner in the rinse.

- A dry towel put in with the clothes in the dryer will absorb moisture and reduce the drying time. Rolling wet clothes in a towel before drying also will remove a lot of moisture and save on electricity.

HAND WASHING—THE RIGHT WAY

Hand washing is preferable to machine washing for nylons, sweaters, and delicate fabrics and garments.

- Before putting clothes in the water make sure the detergent or soap has dissolved completely.
- Soak clothes, except for woolens, for about two hours before hand washing to loosen the dirt.
- Squeeze clothes gently through the fingers. Don't rub hard. Wool should never be rubbed.
- Use a soft brush to loosen dirt around collar and cuffs, but only if necessary.

Hand washing—the lazy way

- There's no really lazy way of hand washing. Follow the instructions above.
- After hand washing some items can be rinsed in the washing machine using a suitable rinse cycle. Some machines have a special rinse and short spin cycle for delicate hand-washed items.

Hand washing—the green way

- Use bar soap and some washing soda dissolved in hot water instead of detergent—this is very good for washing with.
- Add a tablespoon of white vinegar to the rinsing water to prevent soap scum.

SOME SPECIAL CASES

Blankets
Non-wool blankets can be washed in the washing machine, according to the material. Otherwise, take them to be dry-cleaned.

Comforters
Comforters filled with synthetic fiber can be washed in the washing machine. Feather-filled comforters also can be washed at home, in a cool, short wash. From time to time, fluff them up while they are drying. Otherwise there are specialists who will clean feather-filled comforters.

Crepe fabrics
These may shrink after washing. Iron while still very damp and pull the fabric gently against the iron while you work.

Curtains
Wash curtains or have them cleaned at least once a year, following the manufacturer's care instructions. Test for color-fastness before washing (see page 5).

- Remove curtain hooks and weights before washing.
- Wash delicate fabrics by hand.
- If the curtains are lined, wash as for the "weakest" fabric or it may shrink. Otherwise have them cleaned professionally.
- See page 26 for net curtains.

Drip-dry clothes
Don't use bleach on polished cottons as it may combine with the polishing agent and then can't be rinsed out.

Elastic and elasticized garments
Don't wash in hot water. Don't wring or pull. Roll in a towel to remove excess moisture.

Feather pillows

Immerse in a bath or tub of tepid water with 1 ounce of washing soda. Rinse through by lifting up and allowing to drain and then immersing again. Do this three or four times in fresh water without soda. You can use soap flakes for the wash, and if you do, soften the first rinse water with half a cup of white vinegar to ensure removal of all soap.

Knitted clothes

Wool should never be rubbed or moved around too much in water because of the scales on the wool fiber which felt up and shrink the fabric. Man-made knits can stretch badly, so wash them in the same way as wool, then pull into shape and dry flat. Use warm water and squeeze the garment in your hands—don't rub. Squeeze gently then roll up in a towel to get rid of excess moisture.

Lace

Store carefully and wash as seldom as possible. Soak in warm water then hand wash in hand-hot water.

- Don't wash lace of different colors together.
- Delicate lace should be pinned on to a linen-covered board and sponged gently with soapy water, then left to dry on the board.
- Don't use bleach on delicate lace.

Linens that have gotten musty

Add 3 tablespoons baking soda to each quart of boiling water. Boil for 5 minutes, then wash as usual.

Mildew

Treat while fresh.

- Wash thoroughly and dry in the sun.
- Or sponge with white vinegar before washing and soak in a solution of 1 teaspoon bleach to 1 quart of warm water.

Shower curtains
Wash in cool cycle of washing machine adding a little detergent and bleach. Put two old white bath towels in with the wash. Add one cup of white vinegar to the rinse water. Do not spin dry. See also page 88.

Soft toys
Wash fairly often in warm water and soap flakes and rinse thoroughly. Wash dark colors separately. Wrap in a towel to soak up excess moisture. Hang (by the ears if it's a stuffed animal) to dry.

Ties
Get professionally cleaned.

White cotton socks
Add a slice of lemon to the water and boil them for 5 minutes to restore whiteness.

STARCHING

Starch stiffens limp fabrics but also helps to keep out dirt, and most fabrics wear better when starched. The soft glossy finish it gives cottons holds down the fine surface hairs and fills the gaps between fibers where dust and dirt collect. Too much starch, however, can cause dryness and cracking of the fabric.

Starch comes in liquid, powder, or spray form. Always follow the manufacturer's instructions.

Spray starch can be sprayed on fabrics just before ironing. It's the most convenient type of starch to use.

IRONING—THE RIGHT WAY

- Let the iron warm up for 5 minutes after you've turned it on. This will give the thermostat time to settle and the sole plate time to heat up evenly.

- Start with the items that need the coolest setting, such as silk and acetate, and increase the heat as you get to the more robust cottons and linens. Always follow any instructions on the label.

- Pull napkins, handkerchiefs, etc., into shape before you iron them.

- Tack pleats in place before ironing.

- Press embossed cottons on the wrong side.

- Very dry, creased fabric should be generously splashed with water and rolled up for a couple of hours before ironing to let the moisture spread through the fibers.

- A spray bottle is useful for spraying moisture on to dry fabrics if you have not got a steam iron.

Ironing a shirt

1. Iron the collar, starting at the points and working toward the back.
2. Iron the cuffs.
3. Iron the sleeves, starting at the underarm seams. Run the point of the iron into the gathers at the cuff and work up toward the shoulder.
4. Iron one front and work around to the other front. Hang the shirt to air before folding.
5. Fold sides to middle, fold arms back. Fold bottom to top, arms inside.

Ironing pants

1. Iron pockets.
2. Fit the top part of the pants over the end of the ironing board and iron.
3. Fold pants lengthwise, seams to the middle, creases at the outside edges. Iron the inside and then outside of the leg.
4. Turn pants over and iron the other leg in the same way.

Ironing sheets

Fold the sheets in four, lengthways. Iron the outside surfaces, then turn the folds inwards and iron again.

Ironing—the lazy way

- Fold T-shirts and sweatshirts when still slightly damp, smooth flat and dry in a warm place. They won't need ironing at all.

- Pull damp sheets hard at each corner (you need two people for this), fold, smooth, and dry on a warm surface. They shouldn't need ironing.

- Putting pants in a press is a good alternative to ironing them.

- Buy items made of easy-care, drip-dry fabrics that don't need ironing.

- Iron only the parts that will be seen (e.g. the top of a sheet).

Ironing—the green way

The lazy way is also the green way as you use up less energy. See above.

PRESSING

Pressing is an ironing technique used on tweed suits, wool, and other items that are too heavy to iron satisfactorily or that might singe, or get shiny if ironed. Use a hot iron and a clean, damp, lint-free cloth—a tea towel works well or a bit of old but clean cotton sheet.

1. Place the garment on the ironing board with the damp cloth on top.
2. Press the iron down then lift it and press it again. Don't slide it over the cloth. Continue until the cloth is dry and the garment flat. If necessary dampen the cloth again at intervals.
3. Air the clothes well after pressing and before hanging them in a closet.

- If you have a steam iron, you can press very lightweight fabrics under a dry cloth.
- When pressing pleats, tack them in place first, EXACTLY on the crease line.

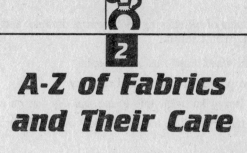

A-Z of Fabrics
and Their Care

Every material whether natural or man-made has characteristics that require special treatment. For instance, rayon becomes weak while it is in water so it should not be soaked for too long; many synthetics will acquire permanent creases if they get too hot when wet, and wool shouldn't be rubbed in water or it will shrink.

The following is a list of the most commonly used fabrics and fibers and is intended as a quick reference guide on how to care for them.

Acetate

Man-made cellulose acetate fiber usually of wood pulp. Quite silk-like in appearance; colorfast; won't shrink.

- Warm wash, gentle cycle, cold rinse.
- Do not wring or twist.
- Drip-dry or roll in a towel to remove excess moisture.
- Iron while still damp with a cool iron.
- Knitted acetates should be given a cold rinse and short spin.
- Don't use acetic acid, acetone, alcohol, or similar chemicals for stain removal or the fabric will dissolve.

Acrylic
By-products of oil refining. Soft, warm, durable, and mildew-resistant. Won't shrink.

- Warm wash, cold rinse, short spin.
- Rinse pleated garments and drip-dry.
- Pull heavy knitwear into shape and dry flat on a towel.
- Pile fabrics may be brushed lightly with a soft brush when dry.
- Some garments need to be ironed lightly with a cool iron once the garment is dry.

Angora
Fluffy rabbit wool used for sweaters, hats, scarves, etc. Very soft with characteristic white hairs. Sometimes mixed with nylon.

- Hand wash and treat as for wool.

Astrakhan
Lamb's skin or imitation lamb's skin.

- Treat as sheepskin: dry-clean or shampoo or wash as for wool.
- No need to iron.

Bonded fibers (nonwoven fabric)
Off-white, crush resistant, porous, water-repellent and light. Used for interlinings.

- Warm wash; don't rub.
- Roll loosely in a towel to absorb moisture.
- Don't spin or wring.

Braid
Used to decorate some garments.

- Dry-clean only. Sprinkle with baking soda, leave, then brush off with a fine wire brush.
- Or make a paste of denatured alcohol and French chalk (see page 171) to remove tarnish.
- Or use a mixture of cream of tartar and dry bread, apply when dry and brush lightly with a clean, soft brush.

Brocade
May be acetate, cotton, silk, rayon, or a mixture.

- Dry-clean only. Too heavy to handle when wet.

Broderie anglaise
Openwork embroidered fabric of white cotton or cotton/polyester.

- Wash as for cotton, but make sure other garments have no hooks to catch in the embroidery.

Buckram
Cotton stiffening fabric treated with size.

- Dry-clean only.

Calico
Medium-weight cotton.

- Wash as for cotton.
- Put splash of mineral spirits into the first wash of unbleached calico to remove starch and whiten fabric.

Cambric
Handkerchief cotton.

- Wash as for cotton.

Camel hair
Expensive, soft, warm brown wool.

- Dry-clean only.

Candlewick
Tufted fabric of nylon, polyester, rayon, triacetate, or cotton.

* Wash as for fiber concerned.

Canvas or duck
Very stiff cotton used for tents and yacht sails, handbags, and shoes.

* Scrub with a block of soap and a scrubbing brush then pour buckets of water over it to rinse.

Cashmere
Light, soft wool from the cashmere goat. Scarce and expensive.

* Wash as for wool.

Chenille
Fabric with soft, velvety pile. May be cotton, rayon, wool or silk.

* Wash or dry-clean according to fiber.

Chiffon
Sheer fabric with soft, rippled finish. May be silk, rayon, or other man-made fibers.

* Wash as for fiber concerned.
* Don't wring.
* When almost dry, iron gently and patiently with cool iron. Stretch garment gently in all directions then into its correct shape as you iron.

Chintz
Cotton fabric with a shiny side.

* Dry-clean.

- If you DO wash use starch or a plastic stiffener unless the glaze is permanent.

Corduroy
Also pin whale and wide whale. Can be cotton, cotton/rayon, or cotton/polyester.

- Wash as for the more delicate fiber.
- Occasionally smooth the pile as it dries and shake it from time to time. Should then need no ironing.
- If you must iron, press gently while still damp on the wrong side with several thicknesses of folded material between the garment and the iron.

Cotton
Cotton fabrics are absorbent and tough, washable, and hang well.

- Wash white cotton in hot water.
- Test colored cottons for fastness. Safest to wash reds with reds, blues with blues, and so on, anyway.
- Always follow any instructions on the label especially for delicate cottons such as voile, organdie, or drip-dry and stain-repellent fabrics.

Crepe
Fabric with wrinkled, crinkled surface.

- Wash in hand-hot water. Roll in a towel to absorb excess moisture.
- Iron on the wrong side with warm iron while still damp or use steam iron.

Damask
Woven patterned fabric, can be cotton, silk, wool, rayon, or a mixture.

- Treat as for weakest fiber. See care label.

Denim
Heavy cotton; also available in rayon/cotton mixture.

- Wash as for weakest fiber.
- Denim will shrink slightly unless preshrunk.

Elastomers (e.g., spandex, Lycra)
Materials mostly based on polyurethane, which have the elasticity of rubber.

- Follow the care label or hand wash in warm water or machine wash, gentle cycle.
- Rinse or roll in a towel; drip-dry.
- Don't iron.

Faille
Fine ribbed fabric. May be silk, cotton, or man-made fiber.

- Treat as for fiber concerned.

Felt
Matted woolen material. Shrinks easily.

- Don't wash.
- To clean at home, make a paste with mineral spirits and French chalk. Rub in well and let it dry, then brush it off.

Flannel
See wool.

Flannelette
Heavy-weight brushed cotton fabric used for winter sheets and nightgowns.

- Wash as for cotton.

Foulard
Usually acetate, may be silk.

- Wash according to fiber.

Fur fabric (fake fur)
May be of nylon, rayon, cotton, acrylic, or polyester.

• Cotton and rayon should be dry-cleaned.

• Others may be washed according to fiber or to the instructions on the label. If in doubt, wash as nylon.

• Or lightly sponge fur fabric with warm water and detergent, sponge, rinse, and dry with a towel.

Gabardine
Strong, woven fabric twilled with diagonal ribs. Can be of cotton, worsted, or blends of those and man-made fibers.

• Dry-clean.

Georgette
Delicate, sheer fabric a bit like crepe. Can be of wool, cotton, silk, or man-made fibers.

• If silk or wool, get garment professionally cleaned.

• Wash man-made fabrics according to weakest fiber or follow the instructions on the label.

• Test for colorfastness (see page 5).

Gingham
See Cotton.

Grosgrain
Finely ribbed fabric. May be from various fibers.

• Wash or dry-clean according to fiber or the care label.

Jersey
Stretchy, knitted fabric in stockinette stitch. Can be of wool, silk, cotton, nylon, or other man-made fibers.

• Wash or dry-clean according to the care label.

• No care label? Get the garment dry-cleaned.

Kapok

From seed pods of the kapok tree. Waterproof, light, fluffy, resilient. Used for stuffing mattresses and cushions. Liable to get lumpy in the wash.

- Dry-clean only.

Lace

Can be cotton, polyester, nylon, or a mixture.

- Wash according to fiber. Use a soap or detergent specially formulated for delicate fabrics.
- Old lace should be put in a pillowcase to be washed.
- Curtain lace should be washed in hot water and soap flakes. If cotton, boil in a pot on the stove from time to time.
- Pull into shape while drying.
- Iron with a hot iron on the wrong side.
- For delicate handmade lace see page 12.

Lamé

See Metallic yarns.

Lawn

Fine fabric of cotton, polyester/cotton or rayon/cotton blends.

- Hand wash or give the article a very short, gentle machine wash.
- Use hand-hot water, rinse thoroughly, and wring or spin.

Leather gloves

- Wash the gloves while on your hands in warm water and soap flakes.
- Pale-colored gloves should be washed each time they are worn.
- Leave some soap in the gloves after washing. This will

help keep the leather supple. (Synthetic detergent will not give the same result.)

- Dry over wooden or wire hands or, if you don't have any, over a bottle.
- When they are dry, rub the leather between your fingers to soften it.

Leather shoes

- Wet leather shoes should be stuffed with newspaper and dried away from direct heat. A little castor oil rubbed into the uppers and soles after they have dried will soften them and recondition the leather.
- Polish leather shoes frequently (see page 148).

Linen

Woven from fibers of the flax plant. Similar to cotton but with a better texture and longer life.

- Hot wash, rinse thoroughly, tumble dry. Remove from dryer while still damp.
- Iron on the wrong side with hot iron while still damp unless you have an iron with spray steam for bad creases.

Metallic yarns

Non-tarnishable aluminum threads coated with plastic and woven with other yarns.

- Dry-clean only.

Modacrylic

Modified acrylic, similar to acrylic but not as strong.

- Machine or hand wash in warm water and detergent; rinse well.
- Drip-dry.
- If necessary iron with a cool iron.

Mohair
See Wool.

Moiré
See Silk.

Mungo
See Wool.

Muslin
Thin, loosely woven cotton.

- Machine or hand wash in warm water; rinse well.
- Iron while damp with warm iron. Starch.

Net
Fine mesh material. Can be of cotton, nylon, polyester, etc. Cotton net may shrink when washed for the first time.

- Curtain nets should be washed often; once really dirty it's impossible to get them clean.
- Shake first, then rinse in cold water. Wash in soap flakes and hot water. Wash twice if necessary.
- Do not rub, twist, or wring; just squeeze suds gently through fabric.
- If curtains have gotten gray, try washing with Chlorox 2 or soak for a while in soap flakes and water.
- As a last resort, try soaking in regular laundry detergent.
- Net on dresses should be hand washed in warm water and soap flakes. Rinse; drip-dry and iron with a warm iron while still a little damp.

Nylon
Strong, elastic, does not lose its strength when wet; lightweight, absorbs little moisture, flame resistant, resistant to most oils and chemicals, moths, and molds.

- Wash in hand-hot water, cold rinse, short cycle, drip-dry.

Its basic state is gray, and the white pigment will come out if you use hot water. Supermarkets sell nylon whiteners that you can use in the rinse water.

- Don't use bleach.
- Don't expose nylon to direct heat or sunlight.
- Shouldn't need ironing. If it does, use a warm setting when almost dry. Never iron pleated nylon.
- Dip pleated garments up and down in soap and water.
- Wash pleated and delicate garments every time you use them; once really dirty the dirt won't come out.
- If taken for dry-cleaning, mark clearly "Nylon."
- Nylon fur with an interlining should not be washed but given a wet shampoo. Mix some liquid detergent in warm water and sponge the lather into the fur only. Treat a small patch at a time and don't wet the lining or interlining. Rinse with a clean, not-too-wet sponge and pat dry with a towel. Or use a dry shampoo.

Organdie

Permanently stiffened delicate fabric. Can be cotton or nylon.

- Squeeze gently in hand-hot water and mild detergent; rinse well.
- Wring and hang to dry.
- Iron on the right side while still damp.
- Limp organdie can be rinsed in a quart of warm water with one tablespoon borax.
- Nylon organdie should be washed as nylon.

Organza

Sort of stiffened chiffon. May be silk or various fibers.

- Wash according to fiber and handle with care.

Polyester

From by-products of petrol refining. Very strong whether wet or dry. High resistance to abrasion; sheer, lightweight. Won't shrink or stretch. Resistant to moths and mildew. Often combined with cotton.

- Hand or machine wash, cold rinse, normal cycle. Tumble-dry.
- Loosen bad stains by impregnating them with concentrated detergent, leaving for 15 minutes then laundering as usual.
- Wash pleated garments by hand and hang to drip-dry.

Poplin
Can be cotton, rayon, silk, or wool.

- Wash as for relevant fiber.

PVC
Strong man-made plastic material.

- Hand-wash only; drip-dry only. Do not iron.

Rayon
Man-made fiber of wood pulp. Weak when wet, strong when dry. Can look like silk, linen, wool, or cotton but should be treated more gently.

- Hand-wash frequently in warm water.
- Don't twist, wring, or pull while washing.
- Iron with steam iron or while still damp.
- Iron shiny fabrics on right side, matt fabrics on wrong side.

Repp
Heavy woven fabric. Can be cotton or mixture of cotton and man-made fibers.

- Treat as for weakest fiber. See care label.

Sateen
Satin-like fabric. May be cotton or rayon.

- Treat as for weakest fiber.

Satin
Smooth, slippery material with short nap. Can be silk, cotton, polyester, nylon, or acetate.

- Wash lightweight satins according to fiber. Press on wrong side, while still damp, until completely dry.
- Acetate satin should be ironed on the wrong side with a cool iron while evenly damp. Do not sprinkle with water or it will spot.
- Dry-clean heavier satins.

Seersucker
Crinkled lightweight fabric. Can be cotton, silk, nylon, or polyester.

- Wash as for the fiber.
- Needs no ironing.

Serge
Suit fabric in worsted or blends of wool and rayon or other fibers.

- Dry-clean or wash quickly in warm water; squeeze out water and dry away from direct heat.
- Press under a damp cloth with a warm iron.

Shantung
Chinese silk with slubs. May also be acetate or nylon.

- Wash as appropriate for the fiber.

Sharkskin
Smooth woven or knitted fabric, may be cotton or more usually acetate.

- Wash as for the fiber.
- May show watermarks if ironed over damp patches so dry evenly and don't iron until almost dry.

Sheepskin

Wool from sheep; or may be acrylic.

- Dry-clean only.

Silk

Silk does not conduct heat, so it keeps in the heat of the body and is warm to wear. It is also strong, resilient, elastic, and wrinkle resistant. Sunlight and perspiration can weaken it, however.

- Silk taffetas and brocades should be dry-cleaned.
- Wash garments every time you wear them or perspiration stains may be impossible to remove and may weaken the fabric.
- Other stains should be removed professionally, but tell the cleaner what the stain is.
- Don't soak in regular laundry detergent. Use a handwash product according to the manufacturer's instructions.
- Iron while still damp with a cool iron or a steam iron.
- Bleach white silk with a solution of 1 part hydrogen peroxide and 8 parts water.
- Silk stockings last longer if soaked in clean, cold water before you wear them. After wearing wash in lukewarm water and detergent. Squeeze gently, don't rub.
- If you wash colored silks immerse the garments in a solution of 2 teaspoons strong acetic acid (or white vinegar) to 6 pints water after the final rinse. Leave for a few minutes then dry without rinsing. This is to ensure the colors won't be affected by any alkali in the detergent.
- Don't rub silk while it is wet or the filaments break up and produce a white, chalky effect.

Taffeta

Plain, shiny, close-woven fabric, may be of silk, wool, acetate, polyester, or nylon.

- Most taffetas should be dry-cleaned. Nylon may be washed.

Terylene
See Polyester.

Ticking
Striped closely woven cotton material used to cover mattresses and pillows and to keep the feathers in.

- Wash as for cotton.

- When dry, rub the inside with beeswax as an extra barrier for the feathers.

Triacetate
A material of cellulose acetate fibers, made from wood pulp and cotton. Can be embossed or permanently pleated, resists dirt and creasing, won't shrink or stretch, can be woven or knitted and dries quickly. Often blended with other fibers.

- Hand wash in warm water and detergent, swirl gently but don't squeeze. Drip-dry.

- If machine washing give short, warm wash with cold rinse.

- If necessary use a cool iron.

- Triacetate can be dry-cleaned with perchloroethylene.

- Don't use acetone, acetic acid, or alcohol as stain removers or the fabric will dissolve.

Tricot
Jersey fabric made of rayon, nylon, or polyester.

- Wash as appropriate for fiber.

Tulle
Fine net of cotton, rayon, nylon, or other fibers.

- Wash as for fiber.

- If the net becomes limp, dip cotton tulle in weak starch; dip nylon and rayon tulle in a gum arabic solution.

Tweed
Heavy-twilled woolen fabric. Sometimes polyester or acrylic.

- Dry-clean woolen tweeds.
- Wash according to fiber.

Velour
Fabric with a heavy pile, usually acrylic but may be other man-made fibers or cotton or silk.

- Dry-clean.

Velvet
Pile fabric of silk, cotton, wool, rayon, nylon, etc. Many are uncrushable, spot-proof, and easily washed.

- Wash according to fiber.
- Shake occasionally while drying and smooth the pile with a soft cloth or a velvet brush.
- Or dry-clean.

Vicuna
See Wool.

Viscose
See Rayon.

Voile
Sheer woven material may be of cotton, rayon, nylon, or polyester.

- Wash as appropriate for fiber.

Wool
Natural fiber from the coats of sheep, lambs and goats, or camels. Special sorts of wool are made from the alpaca,

llama, vicuna, camel, goat, and rabbit. Wool has a coating of scales that work against each other if the wool is rubbed while wet, and this causes the fibers to shrink and "felt." Wool also stretches when wet (but will never "unfelt"). Wool absorbs moisture, is resilient, elastic, and resists wrinkling.

- Hand wash unless the care label says it's machine washable. Squeeze the garment gently; never rub, twist, or wring. Use a specially formulated wool detergent for use in cold water (such as Woolite).

- Never tumble-dry wool.

- Lay the garment flat on a towel and pull gently into correct shape, then leave to dry.

- Yellowed white wool can be soaked in a solution of 1 part hydrogen peroxide to 10 parts water. Rinse in warm water.

- Or dry-clean.

3
Stain Removal at Home

This chapter deals with how to tackle stains on fabrics using one of the four basic stain removing techniques: absorbing, flushing through, using solvents, or bleaching. Understanding the reason for the different techniques involved enables you to work out for yourself how to treat stains and fabrics.

HOME STAIN-REMOVAL KIT

Have an emergency stain-removal kit in the home so that you can deal with stains straightaway. This gives the best chance of success.

Keep everything well labeled and out of the reach of children. A well-stocked emergency kit should contain the following items:

- Spray bottle for spraying cold water
- White tissues, small sponges, and white, absorbent cotton (cotton wool)
- Salt
- Medicine dropper for application of powerful solvents (don't *store* solvent in it though)
- Fuller's earth, French chalk, or talcum powder

- Baking soda
- Household bleach (chlorine bleach)
- Hydrogen peroxide
- Sodium perborate (non-chlorine bleach, such as Clorox 2)
- Household ammonia
- Amyl acetate (or non-oily nail polish remover)
- Commercial dry-cleaning solvent
- Mineral spirits
- White vinegar (acetic acid)
- Lemon juice (citric acid)
- Margarine, glycerine
- An ironing board makes a good work bench.

ABSORBING

Use this for wet things spilled on fabric and carpets before the stain dries, and also to get rid of greasy particles in fur and other unwashable fabrics. There are various suitable absorbents:

Salt
This will absorb urine, fruit juice, and red wine. Pour a generous amount on to carpet, tablecloth, etc., and leave for several hours to soak up the liquid. Then vacuum or shake out and dry-clean, launder or shampoo (carpets and rugs).

Tissues
Use white tissues to absorb the liquid if you have no salt. Place several on to the stain and step on them gently. Don't rub. When the tissues become saturated, remove them and apply fresh ones.

Fuller's earth, French chalk, and talcum powder
All of these will absorb grit and dirt from fur, felt, etc., in the

same way that dry shampoos clean hair. Shake on to the garment. Leave for 12 hours or so. Brush out gently but thoroughly.

FLUSHING THROUGH— THE RIGHT WAY

Use this method for liquids, fruit juices, wine, and non-greasy stains on washable fabrics. Cold water is still one of the best stain removers.

- Use cold water or cold water and liquid detergent for non-greasy stains.

1. Lay the fabric face down on an absorbent pad of paper tissue or cotton wool or white, lint-free cloth. This will help to draw out the stain.
2. Use a spray bottle to force water through just the stain. Some stains may respond to straight liquid detergent being squirted through the fabric and left for a little while before flushing out.
3. When the stain is dissolved, flush with water from well outside the stained area, working toward the center, using a spray bottle with a fine spray or a medicine dropper.
4. Rinse thoroughly and wash as usual.

- Don't use water on dyed raw silk, or moiré patterns, which show up on only the right side of the fabric.

Flushing through—the lazy way

- Leave the stained part of the garment soaking in cold water or water and detergent for an hour or two then rinse thoroughly before laundering as usual. Don't try this lazy way on special clothes or delicate fabrics.

Flushing through—the green way

- Use as little of all household detergents and solvents as you can.

- Use liquid detergents without phosphates or perfumes.

- Use *very* little bleach, and leave it to work for longer than usual.

- Soda water will flush out red wine if you catch it right away. If using on a carpet, mop up well between applications so as not to get the carpet too wet.

USING SOLVENT—THE RIGHT WAY

Use on grease, oil, or stains that have a greasy base, such as milk, cream, sauce, lipstick, etc.

The most common solvents, sold as spot removers under various trade names, are trichloroethane and perchloroethylene. Commercial stain removers may be in liquid, aerosol, or paste form. Other useful solvents are mineral spirits, denatured alcohol, or acetone (not for use on acetate fabrics).

- Always follow the manufacturers' instructions where they exist. Many solvents are flammable and/or poisonous, so use them with care.

- Don't use solvents near an open flame or in a closed space.

1. Scrape off as much of any solid matter as you can without damaging the fabric. A blunt knife is a useful tool and usually handy.

2. Put a white cloth or paper tissue under the stain to prevent it from being transferred to another part of the garment.

3. Soak another cloth in solvent and dab in a circle, starting outside the stain and working toward the center.

4. Rinse thoroughly and wash according to the care label or,

if the garment is not washable, air it well or dry gently with a warm hair dryer.

Using solvents—the lazy way

There's no lazy way to remove these kinds of stains—the job must be done at once and with patience. If you can't be bothered or don't feel confident, take the garment to a dry-cleaner as soon as possible.

Using solvents—the green way

- Don't use aerosols.
- Use margarine, glycerine, or white petroleum jelly to soften tar and oil before laundering.
- Use white vinegar instead of a commercial solvent.
- If you do use solvents, don't pour them down the drain. Instead absorb them with a piece of old rag and put them in the garbage.

BLEACHING STAINS— THE RIGHT WAY

Use this treatment for residual stains that remain after you have used other techniques. Use only on white fabrics or very diluted and for a short time on coloreds. See general instructions for bleaching on page 7.

- Before using bleach on colored fabrics always test a small piece of the fabric where it can't be seen (inside the hem or a seam) for colorfastness (see page 5).

For small stains
1. Mix 1 teaspoon chlorine bleach to 1½ pints cold water.

2. Put a clean cloth or a wad of tissue under the fabric exactly below the stain and dab the stain with another cloth moistened with the diluted bleach solution.

3. Rinse the garment thoroughly then wash or dry-clean as usual.

NOTE: Don't splash bleach on the clothes you are wearing, and make sure there's none left in garments after rinsing that could affect other clothes in the wash.

Bleaching whole garments

1. Use 2 teaspoons bleach to 2½ gallons water. Or follow the manufacturer's instructions. Immerse article for 10 to 15 minutes.

2. Rinse thoroughly before washing as usual.

Bleaching stains—the lazy way

Use slightly more bleach than recommended and it will take slightly less time to work.

NOTE: Check garment frequently and don't leave in the stronger solution too long or the fabric will suffer. Use stronger solution bleach only on white articles.

Bleaching stains—the greener way

Use hydrogen peroxide, which is milder than chlorine bleach (see below) and can be used safely on wool and silk.

Using hydrogen peroxide

• Use 1 part peroxide to 8 parts water for bleaching. Items can be soaked for up to 12 hours, but don't soak silk or wool. Before using on rayons and nylons test for colorfastness (see page 5).

• For stubborn stains apply the hydrogen peroxide and water solution with a medicine dropper or a spray bottle directly on to the stain, putting a pad of tissue underneath. Keep adding more bleach solution until the stain disappears. Don't pour peroxide back into the bottle because it is very susceptible to impurities.

Using sodium perborate or non-chlorine bleaches

- Non-chlorine bleaches, also known as peroxy bleaches, contain sodium perborate or potassium monopersulphate. They are milder than chlorine bleach and are safe on all fabrics. Use on textiles with durable-press finishes and for silk and wool.

- Follow manufacturer's instructions.

The sun

Alternatively leave newly washed clothes out in the sun to dry as the sun acts as a bleach.

SOME BASIC STAIN REMOVAL RULES

- Deal with a stain as soon as possible, AT ONCE if you can.

- If you are not sure what created a stain, or what the fabric content of the garment is, take the garment to a professional cleaner.

- Scrape off any solid matter at once with a blunt knife or, if it has dried, loosen it with a solvent or pat it with a stiff bristle brush (don't use a brushing action).

- Fabrics with special surfaces like taffeta, velvet, or satin should always be cleaned professionally or you may ruin the surface effect.

- Hold the fabric stain-down so the stain will go out the way it came in rather than trying to push it right through the fabric.

- Keep a pad of clean, white tissue or cotton material underneath the stained area to absorb stain remover and stain.

• Don't apply heat to the fabric in any form before tackling a stain. Many foods contain albumen or similar protein that is "fixed" by heat. So don't, for instance, wash the garment in hot water or hold it over the steam from a kettle.

• Do test any stain remover on a hidden piece of garment first—the inside hem, for instance, or an inside seam. Some treatments may make the colors run or fade, and some may damage the fibers.

• Don't try to remove the last traces of stubborn stains. It's often better to wear the thing with a residual stain barely showing than risk ruining the fabric by applying too much solvent or overzealous rubbing.

• Dissolve any residual stain in a suitable fluid (water, water and detergent, or solvent).

• Upholstery and carpets must be sponged and dabbed dry alternately so they don't get too wet. Don't let the liquid get into any padding or backing, where it may do irreparable damage. (See pages 101–102).

• When the stain has dissolved, start flushing with water or solvent well outside the stained area, moving round and working toward the center. A plastic bottle with a fine spray nozzle is good for this.

• If you have used solvent, blot up any excess with a clean, dry cloth or sponge and drive off any remaining with a stream of warm air from a hair dryer, using a circular motion, as when cleaning.

• If you used bleach or detergent, finish by rinsing thoroughly and washing the garment as usual.

• Always rinse the area well between types of treatment if the first attempt doesn't work.

• Never mix solvents before use.

Testing for colorfastness

Some dyes only remain fixed for a limited time so test all fabrics for colorfastness each time you treat the garment in a new way, especially if you think it will have to spend a long time in contact with the stain removal agent.

1. Make up the cleaning solution in the proportion you intend to use it.
2. Apply it to a hidden piece of the garment.
3. Put the treated area between two pieces of clean white fabric or tissue and press with a warm iron.
4. If any color has been transferred to the white fabric or tissue then it is not colorfast and should be dealt with by a professional.

Final touches

Sometimes powdery particles stay trapped between the fibers after the rest of the stain has dissolved and been flushed away. Don't scrape at these with your fingernail. Deal with them by applying straight liquid detergent and gently working the fabric between your fingers. Then rinse with water three or four times, otherwise any residual detergent will attract dirt again.

• Don't use spirits or solvents on rayon, triacetate, or rainproofed fabrics.
• BE PATIENT: gentle dabbing and rinsing over a long period will work in the end, where brisk rubbing would ruin the cloth.

Spot cleaning checklist

1. Act fast.
2. Scrape off solids.
3. Absorb liquids.
4. Treat the stain with a suitable liquid (water, water and detergent, or solvent).
5. Treat any residual stain with bleach (fabric permitting.)

4

A-Z of Stains

The advice in this chapter relates to stains on fabrics and carpets and is based on the basic rules and techniques in Chapter 3.

It is possible to buy a range of commercial products formulated for specific stains. Some of these are very effective, others less so. They are all relatively expensive and involve the use of chemicals. If you are looking for cheaper or greener stain removers or you have no commercial stain removers handy, here are some tried and true alternative methods for removing the various types of stains.

Acids
Flush at once with cold water. Acids do not necessarily stain fabrics, but they are quite likely to destroy them. Even a weak acid will damage fibers, especially cotton, linen, nylon, rayon, and colored materials. When flushed, neutralize any acid left with household ammonia (diluted as directed on the bottle) or baking soda dissolved in a little water. Rinse well.

Adhesives
If you get any commercial adhesive where you did not intend to, check the label or packaging for advice. The manufacturers will often offer advice if you call them or write to them. Here are some specific types of glue and how to deal with them. Remember that some modern glues cannot be removed once they have dried.

Animal and fish glues. Usually soluble in cold water. If not, wet the stain with cold water anyway, treat with household ammonia and rinse. If the stain is still there, wet it again, apply liquid detergent, and rinse.

Household adhesives and model aircraft cement. These are cellulose-based. Use non-oily nail polish remover or acetone on most fabrics except acetate fabrics. (Chemically pure amyl acetate won't damage such fabrics, but as the adhesive has acetone in it the fabric will have been damaged anyway.)

Elmer's Glue. A household glue made of casein (a skimmed milk product). Sponge or soak in cold water. Then work straight liquid detergent into the stain and rinse. An enzyme detergent may work better. If the stain remains, use bleach. On unwashable garments, use a dry-cleaning solvent.

Epoxy adhesives. These consist of a glue and a hardener mixed together just before use. They can be removed with denatural alcohol spirits before they set. Once hardened, it's impossible to remove them.

Polyvinyl acetate. (PVA and filled PVA) Clean off with denatured alcohol.

Synthetic rubber adhesives. (Contact adhesives.) Use non-oily nail polish remover or acetone except on acetate fabrics in which case use pure amyl acetate. Then flush with a dry-cleaning solvent.

Rubber-based adhesives. Try an oil paint thinner or write to the manufacturer who may have a commercial product. Don't use paint strippers, which are too harsh.

Sticky labels and sticky tape. Soak, or keep covered with a wet cloth. Rub with methylated or mineral spirits.

Superglues. These "bond in seconds" and are quite difficult to use. If fingers, eyelids, etc., get stuck together, don't panic. The glue is activated by moisture and soluble in moisture. Hold a damp cloth over the spot until it comes unstuck. Fingers can be unstuck by rolling a pencil gently between them. Eyes can be unstuck by holding a damp cotton ball over the eye.

Alcohol
See specific stain (e.g., Wine, Beer, Perfume).

Alkalis (such as washing soda, baking soda)
May permanently damage a fabric, particularly polyester or polyester blends, so wash immediately as for acid. Rinse in cold water and neutralize any last traces with white vinegar. Rinse again.

Anti-perspirants
Treat with dry-cleaning solvent, then household ammonia. Rinse thoroughly.

Ballpoint pen
Most ballpoint ink is soluble in methylated spirit. Flush repeatedly; the stain may be stubborn. Air or rinse the garment thoroughly.

• On suede try rubbing with an abrasive paper, but only gently, and stop if it looks as though the suede will suffer.

Beer
Treat with white vinegar and rinse. Treat with liquid detergent and rinse. If stain persists, treat with hydrogen peroxide (test fabric first) and rinse. If the fabric is washable, wash at high temperature and dry it in the sun to bleach it.

Bird droppings
Soak washable articles in warm detergent solution following the directions on the packet. Treat non-washables with 4 tablespoons household ammonia to 3½ pints water, then with white vinegar and rinse. Or rub with a commercial pre-wash product.

• On canvas covers and awnings, brush with a stiff brush that has been run across a bar of soap and sprinkled with washing soda. Hose well and rinse.

Blood
Soak or flush out the stain with cold salt water, while still wet

if possible. Don't use warm water. If wool, don't rub it, just let the water run through the fabric. If the stain has hardened, brush off as much as possible and soak in a solution of liquid detergent and warm water, or bleach with a hydrogen peroxide solution. Then wash or clean according to fabric.

Butter
Scrape off excess. Wash at high temperature if the fabric is suitable. If not treat with solvent then dry with a hair dryer or wash according to fabric.

Candle wax
Pry off as much as you can. This is easier if you freeze the article for an hour or so then crack the pieces off. Any residue can be sandwiched between sheets of clean brown paper, blotting paper, or tissues and ironed with a warm iron. Last remnants of wax should be dissolved and flushed away with a dry-cleaning solvent. Any color left from the wax should be treated with mineral spirits and rinsed.

Caramel
Flush with cold water, treat with liquid detergent and rinse. If necessary treat with hydrogen peroxide diluted with an equal quantity of water and rinse.

Carbon paper
Treat with undiluted liquid detergent and rinse well. If some stain persists treat with a few drops of household ammonia and then with detergent again. Repeat several times if necessary. On non-washable fabrics, dab with mineral spirits.

Car polish and wax
Treat with a dry-cleaning solvent, then liquid detergent. Rinse.

Chewing gum
Freeze for an hour or so and then crack off in small pieces. If you can't get the garment into the freezer, hold ice cubes

against the gum. Alternatively soften with egg white before laundering or sponge with a dry-cleaning solvent.

• If the gum has gotten caught in someone's hair, rub ordinary cold cream into the gummed-up hair then pull down on the hair strands with an old dry towel so the gum slides off onto the towel.

Chocolate and cocoa

Scrape off residue with a blunt knife. Flush with cold water. Treat with liquid detergent. Rinse. If a slight stain remains, use a dry-cleaning solvent.

Cod-liver oil

Fresh stains are easily removed. Spoon up as much as possible. Sponge on solvent from the back of the stain. Rinse. Old cod-liver oil stains are practically impossible to remove, even with bleach.

• On carpets use a dry-foam carpet shampoo.
• On clothes, sponge with a strong solution of mild detergent and wash as usual.

Coffee and tea

Flush immediately and thoroughly with cold water, rinse in cold water. If necessary soak in hand-hot water and liquid detergent then rinse thoroughly. Any remaining stain can be treated when dry with half-and-half hydrogen peroxide and water solution.

• Milky coffee stains should be soaked in detergent and water and washed according to fabric.
• Coffee spilled on carpets should be squirted immediately with soda water, then given a carpet shampoo (see page 98).

Cosmetics

Treat with dry-cleaning solvent, then a solution of weak

household detergent and water with a few drops of ammonia added. See also Rouge.

Cough medicine
Usually in a base of sugar syrup, so wash out with detergent and water or flush through from the wrong side. Any residual coloring should be treated with diluted household ammonia then mineral spirits or amyl acetate.

Crayon
Dab with solvent and flush any residual color with mineral spirits. More than this will damage the fabric.

Cream
Rinse in cold water, treat with liquid detergent. Rinse.

- On carpets blot up excess or scrape it off. Use a little dry-cleaning solvent and then a dry-foam carpet shampoo.

Crude oil and creosote
Soften with mineral spirits so that you can scrape away as much solid matter as possible. Then flush with a dry-cleaning solvent.

Curry
Soak in diluted household ammonia or mineral spirits. Bleach if the fabric will take it.

Dark soda pop (Coke or Pepsi)
Flush with cold water. Treat from the back with a liquid detergent. Rinse. For residual stains, treat with mineral spirits containing a drop or two of white vinegar then rinse.

Dyes
Wipe up any splashed or spilled dye immediately with tissues. Rinse immediately with cold water. Don't use hot water, which "fixes" many dyes. Then treat with liquid detergent and rinse. Treat again with diluted household ammonia and rinse again. Then treat with mineral spirits or amyl acetate.

- Non-washable items should be professionally dry-cleaned as soon as possible.

- Remember that removing unwanted dye may also remove colors already on the garment, so don't expect the impossible.

Egg
Flush with cold water. Treat with liquid detergent and water. Rinse. Allow to dry and if necessary treat with a dry-cleaning solvent. Soak stubborn stains on white garments in diluted hydrogen peroxide (1 part to 6 parts water) to which 5 drops of ammonia have been added. Rinse well.

Fat, cold
Treat as for Butter.

Fat, hot
On cottons, linens, and wool treat with liquid detergent and rinse. Repeat if necessary. Finish off with a dry-cleaning solvent.

- If synthetic clothing gets splashed with hot fat the fibers will be damaged. Do not use dry-cleaning solvent in this case as it may remove the color and leave white spots. Take it to a professional cleaner instead.

Feces
Scrape off any solid matter and absorb as much of the rest as you can. Soak in a solution of borax and water for half an hour. Wash as normal.

Felt-tip pen
Lubricate the stain with household soap or glycerin and wash as usual. Sponge any residual stain with mineral spirits.

Fruit and fruit juices
Flush with cold water, then treat with liquid detergent. Rinse. Treat residual stains with diluted household ammonia fol-

lowed by diluted hydrogen peroxide (1 part to 6 parts water). Rinse again. Wash white cotton or linen at high temperature.

Furniture polish
Treat with dry-cleaning solvent.

Glue
See Adhesives.

Grass and other leafy stains
Treat with mineral spirits. Dry the fabric then treat with liquid detergent and rinse. On washable fabrics rub the stain with a commercial pre-wash product or soak in liquid detergent and water before washing.

Gravy
Wipe off excess then flush, sponge, spray with, or soak in cold water or cold water and detergent. Treat any residual stain with dry-cleaning solvent.

- On carpets use a carpet shampoo.

Grease
Scrape off as much as possible. Treat with a dry-cleaning solvent then dry with a hair dryer or in the fresh air.

- For white cotton or linen, put some washing soda in a bowl of hot water and soak the article. This will emulsify the grease.

- Wash delicate fabrics in a solution of borax and water. Make sure the borax is thoroughly dissolved before immersing the clothes.

- Absorb grease from non-washable items (such as felt hats) with fuller's earth, or French chalk. Mix it to a stiff paste with water, put it on the stain and brush it out gently when dry.

- Or place a piece of blotting paper or tissue above and below the fabric and press with a cool iron. The paper will absorb the grease.

Hair dye

Flush out immediately with cold water, then wash in liquid detergent and water. Put a few drops of household ammonia in the rinse water. Treat residual stains with mineral spirits and then, if necessary, a solution of hydrogen peroxide and water. Rinse thoroughly.

Ice cream

Scrape off excess with a spoon or a blunt knife. Soak in warm water and detergent. Treat any residual greasy stain with dry-cleaning solvent.

Ink

This must be caught at once or the stain will be indelible. As a general rule, flush with cold water immediately, then treat with liquid detergent from the back of the stain. Rinse. Repeat until no more color comes out. Treat remaining stain with lemon juice, then with diluted household ammonia. Rinse thoroughly.

• Dried ink needs an acid to get rid of the stain. Oxalic acid is the most effective. It's deadly poisonous so keep it well-labeled and out of reach of children. Pour boiling water through the stain, then apply the dry powder and spread it around with a matchstick. Pour boiling water through again. Rinse the fabric quickly and thoroughly to prevent the acid rotting it. If the fabric is colored, dissolve the acid in water and dip the fabric in the solution and then into cold water so it won't affect the color. Or use a solution of chlorine bleach and water. Test the fabric first.

Ballpoint ink. See under Ballpoint pen.

Fountain-pen ink. Usually soluble in water. Treat with liquid detergent and rinse two or three times, then treat with liquid detergent solution with a few drops of household ammonia added, and rinse again. If necessary treat with a solution of hydrogen peroxide and water and rinse again.

Ink powder. DO NOT GET IT WET. If dry, it will brush out completely with a soft brush.

Felt-tip ink. See under Felt-tip pen.

Indelible marker. You'll be lucky if you can get this out. Flush two or three times with dry-cleaning solvent then with mineral spirits. Treat any residual stain with liquid detergent containing a little household ammonia. Rinse thoroughly. As a last resort try a solution of hydrogen peroxide and water and a final rinse.

India ink. Treat with dry-cleaning solvent, then mineral spirits followed by liquid detergent and water. Rinse.

Printing ink. Flush with mineral spirits. Treat residual stain with liquid detergent and rinse.

Typewriter ribbon. Flush two or three times with a dry-cleaning solvent then with mineral spirits. Then treat with a little liquid detergent containing a few drops of ammonia and rinse well. If there's still the trace of a stain, bleach with a solution of hydrogen peroxide and water and rinse again.

Iodine
Moisten with water and place in the sun, on a warm radiator, or in the steam from a tea kettle.

- For non-washable fabrics, flush with mineral spirits and rinse. If the stain is on acetate fabric, dilute the spirit with 2 parts water.

Jams and preserves
Flush with cold water. Treat with liquid detergent. Rinse. If necessary treat with mineral spirits. Rinse. If necessary, soak in liquid detergent and water. Rinse.

Lacquer
Treat with amyl acetate as often as necessary to remove the stain. Flush with dry-cleaning solvent.

Leather
Leather dyes often contain tannin and, if they have rubbed off on to other materials, are difficult to remove. Apply straight

liquid detergent to the stain. Rub in well. Repeat and rinse well. Bleach final traces of color with a solution of hydrogen peroxide and water.

- If the garment is wool or an unwashable fabric, don't rub it but flush the detergent through.

Lipstick
See Cosmetics.

Liquor (gin, bourbon, scotch, etc.)
Flush with cold water, treat with isopropyl alcohol. Rinse. Treat residual stains with hydrogen peroxide and water. Rinse.

Mascara
See Cosmetics.

Meat juices
Flush with cold water. Soak in liquid detergent. Rinse. Allow to dry and treat residual stains with dry-cleaning solvent.

Metal polish
Flush with water. Treat with liquid detergent and rinse. If necessary, treat with mineral spirits and rinse again.

Mildew or mold
Wipe books and papers with a clean, soft cloth. Stains can sometimes be bleached out with an ink eradicator. Colors will be bleached out too, of course.

- For fabrics flush with diluted bleach from the wrong side. Rinse. Launder as usual.
- For leather, wipe over with undiluted antiseptic mouthwash. Wipe and rub dry with a soft cloth. Polish.
- For shower curtains rub with a mixture of lemon juice and salt or white vinegar and salt.

  To prevent mildew. Prevention really is better than cure so take the following steps to keep mildew at bay.

- Dry clothes promptly after washing.
- Make your own chemical moisture absorbers by tying several pieces of chalk together and hanging them in the cupboard to absorb moisture.
- Use moisture-repellent sprays on shower curtains, etc.

Milk
Treat as for Cream.

Mineral oil
Treat with dry-cleaning solvent. Rinse. Saturate fabric with water, pour or dab on lemon juice while wet, and rinse again.

Modeling materials (e.g., Plasticine, Playdough)
Pick off as much as possible with fingernails or blunt knife. Use liquid detergent and water or dry-cleaning solvent to remove remnants.

Motor oil
Treat with liquid detergent then flush with a dry-cleaning solvent. Repeat the process several times if necessary.

Mud
Allow to dry. Brush off. Any residual stain can be treated with dry-cleaning solvent, then with mineral spirits followed by liquid detergent, and finally rinsed.

Mustard
Flush with cold water. Treat with liquid detergent. Rinse.

Nail polish
Treat with amyl acetate.

- You can use non-oily nail polish remover or acetone, but not on acetate fabrics.

Ointment
Dab with dry-cleaning solvent. Rinse in cold water. Treat with liquid detergent. Rinse.

Paints and lacquers

Acrylic paint. Absorb with tissues or paper towels. Wash out with detergent and water. Use a dry-cleaning solvent or mineral spirits to remove residue. Test synthetics first.

Cellulose paints. (e.g., model aircraft paints) Treat with cellulose thinners. Do not use on rayon.

Water-based paint. Will wash out easily in cold water while still wet. Once dry it's impossible to remove.

Enamel paint. Treat with mineral spirits or a commercial paint remover while still wet.

Oil paint. Sponge wet paint with mineral spirits or dry-cleaning solvent then rinse. Dried oil paint may be removed with a commercial paint remover. Rinse thoroughly afterwards.

Perfume
Treat with household ammonia straight from the bottle. Rinse thoroughly. Or soak in detergent and water then wash as usual.

• Residual stains can be removed with a solution of hydrogen peroxide and water on wet fabric. Rinse.

Perspiration
Wet the fabric and treat with household ammonia straight from the bottle. Rinse thoroughly. Or try soaking in detergent and water. If the stain persists, wet the fabric again and treat with a solution of hydrogen peroxide and water and rinse.

• If anti-perspirant deodorant is combined with the stain, treat with a dry-cleaning solvent, then use household ammonia as described above.

• If dye is combined with the stain, try treating it with white vinegar.

- Treat white linen and cotton by soaking the stain in ¼ cup of mineral spirits to which 5 drops of household ammonia have been added.

- For silk and wool, use diluted hydrogen peroxide. Sponge the stain or soak for 5 to 15 minutes then rinse thoroughly and wash as usual.

- For rayon, nylon, and polyesters, use diluted liquid bleach. Don't soak viscose garments for long, as they become weak while wet.

Resin
Treat with dry-cleaning solvent or mineral spirits from the wrong side. Test for colorfastness (see page 5). Rinse in cold water. On acetate fabric, dilute the spirits with 2 parts water before using.

Rouge
Treat with dry-cleaning solvent. Repeat two or three times. Rinse and dry then treat with liquid detergent and water followed by household ammonia and water. Rinse.

Rust
Cover the stain with salt. Squeeze lemon juice over the salt and leave for an hour. Rinse well. Repeat several times if necessary. Commercial rust removers may be used on white fabrics.

- Or soak in hydrogen peroxide with a little water.

- Rust is very difficult to remove from woolens and silks.
  Get specialized treatment from a professional launderer or dry-cleaner.

Sauce (e.g., white sauce)
Flush with cold water, treat with liquid detergent and water for the grease. When dry, treat with mineral spirits. Rinse.

Scorch marks
Damp the scorched area with 1 part glycerine to 2 parts wa-

ter, rubbing in the solution with the finger tips. Then soak in a solution of 1 tablespoon borax to 1 pint warm water. Leave it for 15 minutes. Rinse well.

- A traditional cure is to polish the mark with the edge of a beveled coin.

Shiny patches
Dark fabrics show up shine more than light ones.

- Some dry-cleaners offer a de-shining service.
- Gently rub the shiny parts with very fine-grade sand paper.
- A traditional cure for shine is to simmer ivy leaves in water until tender and after brushing the garment, use the liquid for sponging the shiny patches.
- A traditional color restorer for black clothes is to brush them all over with distilled water containing a few drops of household ammonia.

Shoe polish
Treat with a dry-cleaning solvent, then a liquid detergent solution with a few drops of household ammonia added. Rinse. Residual stains may be removed with mineral spirits.

Soft drinks
Treat as for Fruit and fruit juices.

Soot
Sprinkle with salt, wait half an hour, then vacuum.

Tar, bitumen or pitch
Rub with grease such as margarine, lard, or peanut butter, then launder out both tar and grease.

- Or see Crude oil and creosote.

Tarnish
Flush with white vinegar or lemon juice. Rinse well. If the

acid in the tarnish changes the color of a dye, sponge with diluted household ammonia or a solution of baking soda and water.

Tea
See Coffee and tea.

Tobacco
Flush with cold water. Treat with white vinegar and rinse. If necessary, treat with liquid detergent containing a little denatured alcohol. Or treat with diluted hydrogen peroxide. Rinse.

Toothpaste
Flush out with water.

Turmeric
See Curry.

Typewriter ribbon
See Ink.

Unidentified stains
If the garment is washable, rinse it in cold water and then wash as usual.

• Non-washable or delicate garments should be taken to a professional dry-cleaner.

Urine
Flush with cold water immediately. Treat with household ammonia straight from the bottle. Then treat with white vinegar or lemon juice and warm water and detergent. If necessary treat with diluted hydrogen peroxide.

• On carpets, blot between applications with a clean terrycloth towel or paper towels.

Vaseline
See Grease.

Vegetable oil (cooking oil, castor oil, linseed oil, etc.)

Treat with dry-cleaning solvent, several times if necessary. Saturate the fabric with water and treat with mineral spirits with a little vinegar added. Rinse.

Walnut

Stains caused by the outsides of walnuts are virtually impossible to remove. Very fresh stains on white cottons and linens may be boiled in detergent and water. Old stains will leave a gray color that may respond to a strong chlorine or hydrogen peroxide bleach solution.

- Non-washable fabrics cannot be treated at home. The only hope is a professional dry-cleaner.

Watercolor paint

Flush with cold water. Residual stains can be treated with household ammonia straight from the bottle used on wet fabric. Rinse very thoroughly.

- Or wet the fabric and treat with hydrogen peroxide diluted half and half with water. Rinse.

Wax polish

Treat with dry-cleaning solvent then with liquid detergent. Rinse.

Wine

Treat with liquid detergent. Rinse. Apply white vinegar. Rinse. Remove any slight residual stain with hydrogen peroxide diluted half and half with water.

Xerox powder

Brush out powder immediately. As long as it doesn't get wet it should all come out. Don't use solvent.

Zinc ointment

Dampen the stained area. Apply mineral spirits. Leave for a few minutes. Rinse in warm water.

5

Dry-Cleaning

Certain fabrics are unsuitable for washing and should be dry-cleaned. This is because some garments may be made mainly of one fabric but have a lining of another and an interlining of yet another. Or there may be buttons, trimming, and zippers held together by sewing thread, all of which may be unsuitable for washing.

Sometimes care labels specify a particular type of solvent, so always check before you hand a garment over to the cleaner and point this out to them.

Even if the care label does not say so, many washable garments can be dry-cleaned and sometimes dry-cleaning is actually more satisfactory. But if the label says dry-clean only, don't attempt to wash the garment.

If you have any doubt about the fabric or what the stain is or the right procedure to follow, or if the garment is a valuable one, don't risk damaging it. Get clothes to the cleaner as soon as you can. If they are just grubby you don't want them to absorb the dirt, and if they are stained then the sooner you deal with the stain the more likely it will come out completely.

Tell the cleaner what the fabric is made of and what was spilled on it. He or she will have a variety of chemicals to treat specific stains and, just as important, the correct techniques for removing them. Attempting such work yourself may set the stain after which even a professional cleaner won't be able to get rid of it. As one professional said to me: "If in doubt, don't fiddle with it. I'm always getting people who say, 'I have spilled egg on this sheepskin coat. I haven't touched it at all—just held it over the kettle for a bit'; so they've shrunk the leather and cooked the egg. If they'd brought it straight to me they would have got the coat back clean and wearable."

How often should clothes be cleaned?

People are curiously inconsistent. They will wash most of their clothes every few days, but they wouldn't dream of having a suit cleaned more than once or twice a year—whereas suits should be cleaned about once a month or every 15 wearings or so. Silk shirts should be cleaned much more often and so should raincoats, which must be automatically reproofed by the cleaner or they will become permanently discolored.

How dry-cleaning works

Dry-cleaning is not really dry. All dry-cleaning machines use a solvent of some kind that dissolves grease, oil, and wax. In fact a dry-cleaning machine does exactly the same things as a washing-machine but uses a dry-cleaning fluid instead of water. Dry-cleaning should also remove water-soluble stains such as sweat, and stains of food and drink, cooking splashes, mud, blood, oil, and graphite (from getting a coat caught in the car door, for instance).

The solvents
There are four main types of dry-cleaning solvents used by professionals. These are trichloroethane, perchloroethylene, fluorocarbon, and mineral spirits. (Carbon tetrachloride, which used to be common, has been found to be extremely toxic, is not used in commercial machines, and should never be used or even kept in the house.)

The most commonly used solvent is perchloroethylene.

The other commonly used solvent used to be fluorocarbon, which is less powerful and won't start to dissolve buttons or finishes, bindings or interlinings. It has a low boiling point so it can be recycled after use by distillation. Fluorocarbon was the best solvent to use for acrylics and other heat-sensitive fabrics and for suede and leather. It boils at less than the temperature of a cup of hot tea. Unfortunately fluorocarbon is definitely not "green" and is being phased out.

Grease-based stains generally will not come out with solvent alone. A small amount of water in the right form is also needed. With wool, however, water must not be used; and it is very important to make sure the cleaner is aware that a garment is made of wool.

The solvent dissolves oils, waxes, and grease and releases particles of dirt. After 4 to 7 minutes the solvent is drained from the drum and the garment is spun, then rinsed in clean solvent, and given another high speed spin. Warm air is blown into the drum to dry the garments while they tumble. With perchloroethylene the drying temperature is around 140°F, but with fluorocarbon it need only reach 86°F. Detergent is often added during the first part of the process to disperse the water evenly (if water is used at all) and to suspend the dust particles and prevent them from going back into the fabric.

All solvents used in dry-cleaning at present are nonflammable, but they are also anesthetics. Small amounts will give you a headache, make you giddy, and possibly even make you unconscious.

DEALING WITH
PROFESSIONAL DRY-CLEANERS

There is no easy way to find a good cleaner. There are usually plenty to choose from. Find one who will give a personal service where you can get advice direct from the person with the machine and where there may be a mending and button-sewing service on the premises.

If you want a specialist cleaner for a particular item such as a comforter or particularly delicate silk, look in the Yellow Pages for local specialists.

Cleaners can offer a variety of services. Much of the work has to be done by hand, which is why it's quite expensive. "Spotting" is the removal of specific stains from a fabric. It has to be done by skilled personnel with a knowledge of fabrics, chemicals, and what has caused the stain. Some stains come out in the normal cleaning process—any that still show are treated before pressing so they will not be set in. Old stains may be impossible to get rid of. A good cleaner will tell you when this is so.

Steam pressing and shaping also have to be done by hand using a variety of different presses, steam finishes, and specialized small appliances (such as "steam puffs" for shaped garments) and hand irons. Pleats are set by hand; linings and underskirts and all elaborate clothes are ironed by hand. Cleaning personnel usually specialize in suit pressing, pleating, or silk finishing, for instance.

Prices for standard articles or services will be quoted on request. Where articles are of exceptional value or of an unusual nature, cleaners may charge a special price.

Special services

- Many dry-cleaners will do small repairs and alterations. Replacing buttons may be included in the overall cleaning charge or there may be a small extra charge.

- Many cleaners will put in new zippers. Some are better at it than others and prices vary so it pays to shop around.

- Retexturing is a special service. It impregnates the fabric with a dressing that renews the set and the way it will hang. It gives firmer pleats and is specially helpful for old, tired looking clothes. Many clothes don't need retexturing, however. Don't ask for knitted materials, woolens or light-weight fabrics to be retextured. The retexturing fluid may be a crease-resistant or crease-retaining resin or a water-proofing agent.

- Dry-cleaning itself is one of the best methods of moth-proofing but a special treatment can be applied that will give even more protection until the next cleaning.

Things that need special care

Wool

This needs special attention when washing or dry-cleaning. Wool thread has a coating of scales which work against each other when in water, making the garment felt and shrink. This doesn't happen in solvent. The looser the knitting the more the wool is likely to shrink. Once shrunk, wool cannot be unshrunk. Make sure the cleaner knows he or she is dealing with wool so that they won't put water in with the solvent mixture.

Furnishings

- Curtains, down quilts, comforters, pillows, cushions, loose covers, etc., can all be efficiently dealt with by a specialist cleaner.

- Carpets and upholstery can be cleaned for you at home, but cleaning companies sometimes prefer to clean rugs at their shop where they can be treated more thoroughly. They will collect and return the carpet. Most companies will offer a silicone treatment to repel dirt and make future cleaning easier.

- Valuable oriental rugs are best treated by specialists.

- Elaborate valances may have to be cleaned by hand and may even have to be unstitched and sewn up again afterward.

Leather and suede

Leather and suede cleaning are highly specialized. Some cleaners deal with all kinds of leather garments including sheepskin, which goes through a special cleaning process and is dried by special methods, too. Suede and sheepskin are usually finished by spraying with oil to keep the skin supple. Dye may be added to the spray to revive faded colors. Many dry-cleaners subcontract the cleaning of suede and leather to specialists.

- Get suede and sheepskin cleaned as soon as dirt begins to

show around collar and cuffs. If a garment is allowed to get very dirty the chances of a cleaner getting it really clean again are small.

• For an extra charge most cleaners will repair damaged cuffs, collars and pockets. Some will also touch up colors damaged during wear and many will match up buttons too.

• Advise your cleaner if the garment is being cleaned for the first time. Cleaning can highlight the different skins used and a cleaner can retint by spraying.

• After cleaning, store under a clean cotton cloth, never plastic, as leather and suede need to breathe.

Velvets

Although velvets are washable, they dry-clean quite satisfactorily; and because they are so heavy to handle when wet, this is probably the best method of cleaning.

Dry-cleaning—the green way?

Unfortunately the only green way of dry-cleaning is to use solvent-based dry-cleaners as little as possible or not at all. Avoid buying new clothes that have to be dry-cleaned, and don't have washable items dry-cleaned—wash them instead.

6

Guidelines for Housework

Hygiene in the kitchen and bathroom is the most important thing to aim for, and it's not difficult to achieve. This is dealt with in Chapter 7. As far as the rest of the house goes, it should be kept clean and tidy, but don't become obsessed with spotlessness and tidiness at the cost of spending time with family and friends.

MAKING HOUSEWORK EASIER

The best way of dealing with housework is by creating a home where you don't have to do much! The important thing is to provide a basic order in the home so that cleaning is a simple process, not made impossible by underlying chaos. There are various ways of reducing housework.

A convenient place for everything

Having a place for everything will make things easier to put away and find, as well as easier to clean. Here are some storage suggestions:

- Bookcases for books—freestanding or built-in shelves.

- Storage near the stove for pots, pans, and casserole dishes.
- Cup hooks for cups.
- Hanging storage for kitchen implements, telephone, and anything else you can get off tables and work surfaces or out of drawers.
- Boxes, baskets, or shelves for different categories of toys.
- Sensible storage for sewing equipment and other hobbies, e.g., a chest of drawers, a specially designed sewing box, or a collection of baskets.
- Filing boxes for family papers and a spike for unpaid bills.
- Hanging storage for anything you can get off the floor: e.g., iron and ironing board, cleaning equipment, tools, folding chairs.
- Convenient shelves for phone books, cookbooks, pen and pencil holders, china, glass, etc.
- Keep all cleaning products out of the reach of children and not under the kitchen sink.

Don't gather junk

Don't surround yourself with more possessions or furniture than you need or can find room for.

- Throw out worn-out clothes, broken toys, old Christmas cards, useless bits of fabric, ugly furniture. If it's too good to throw away take it to the local charity shop.
- Don't buy odd little flea-market bits of junk unless you have a use or a place for them. If you collect things, make a space where they can be displayed and lit.
- Don't collect electrical gadgets or any other appliances unless you need them. Anything that has remained unused for six months will probably never be used, so throw or give away.

Stop dirt from getting in

If dirt, dust, and soot aren't allowed into the home in the first place, then cleaning will be easier.

• Make sure windows and doors fit tightly and don't allow dust to blow in.

• Install a large doormat or even fitted door matting to help capture much dust and dirt on its way in.

• Suggest that people abandon their shoes at the front (or back) door, especially if you live in the country.

Choose efficient housework tools

Good tools will make housework easier and more pleasant to do. Choose tools that are comfortable to handle, good to look at, and easy to care for.

Obviously what you need will depend on whether you live in a large house with a family and pets or alone in a small apartment. Here's a list of suggestions.

• Vacuum cleaner or carpet sweeper

• Broom

• Floor mop, sponge mop, or other "wet" mop

• Dry mop

• Dustpan and brush (or two brushes—one soft, one hard)

• Cloths: dust cloths, dishcloths, tea towels, paper towels, disposable cloths (such as Handiwipes), chamois or scrim for cleaning windows

• Scouring pads or steel wool

• Toilet brush and holder

• Sponges and dishwashing brushes—useful for cleaning baths, basins, and sinks as well as dishwashing. You should have a separate one for pets' dishes. Use different colors for different uses.

Care of equipment

Properly cared for equipment means efficient and economical equipment with a longer life, so it's worth spending time maintaining it properly.

• It's important to keep all cleaning equipment clean and dry when not in use. This is particularly true of cloths. Dishcloths are the most likely cloths to harbour germs, since they are in contact with old food on plates and may remain moist for some time. Bacteria flourish in the warm and damp atmosphere of kitchens and bathrooms, but they will not survive on cloths if they are allowed to dry out. So it is important to rinse out cloths (including dishcloths, wash cloths, and bath sponges) every time they are used and hang them to dry as quickly as possible. It is more hygienic to use disposable cloths and throw them away frequently than to hang on to fabric cloths that are never quite clean or dry.

• Wash dustpan and brush in warm detergent and water and leave in a warm place to dry, preferably outside. Do this once a month or when they begin to look grubby.

• Wash broom in warm detergent and water once a month or so. If you wish to use it as a cobweb brush, wash it and dry it thoroughly before you do so.

• Change the sponge in a floor mop before it becomes so worn that it scratches the flooring.

• Change the vacuum bag frequently. A full bag is inefficient and makes the motor work too hard. Wipe the outside of the vacuum cleaner with a cloth wrung out in detergent and water.

• Empty carpet sweepers after each use. The little boxes don't hold much, but they do pick up a lot.

• Regularly check cords and plugs on electrical equipment for wear. Replace if necessary.

• Rinse mop heads thoroughly and dry completely before putting away.

- Hang brooms, mops, and anything else that will hang on a wall rather than allow them to stand on their bristles.
- New brooms last longer if the bristles are dipped in cold salted water before use. But don't do this to nylon or plastic bristles.
- Clean the broom cupboard occasionally: take everything off the walls and shelves and brush down with the broom before cleaning the walls with a solution of mild disinfectant or vinegar. Leave the door open while you allow the surfaces to dry.

How often should you clean what?

There are no hard and fast rules about this. Here are some guidelines.

Daily

- Wash pet dishes and clean out cat litter boxes.
- Empty ash trays.
- Make beds and put clothes away.
- Clean toilets and bathroom and kitchen sinks.
- Put garbage in plastic bags, tie tops, and put in trash.
- Rinse out cloths and hang in a warm, dry place.
- Clean up any spills and sweep or vacuum if and when necessary.

Weekly (or as necessary)

- Vacuum living areas (some people do this daily).
- Wipe out refrigerator and throw away old food.
- Do the laundry.
- Shake out pets' bedding and clean bird cages.
- Sweep front steps and back yard.
- Change bed sheets.

Monthly

- Clean windows and mirrors.
- Polish silver and metalware.
- Thoroughly clean the stove.
- Clean trashcan.
- Clean filters in washing machine and dryer.
- Clean radiators (winter).
- Give one room in the house a thorough cleaning.

Twice a year

- Defrost refrigerator (even if it's an automatically defrosting one).
- Clean coffee machine, teapot and steam iron if you live in a hard water area.
- Clean out gutters and drains.
- Polish wooden furniture.
- Clean out cupboards and take worthwhile unwanted things to a charity shop or homeless shelter.

Once a year

- Spring clean the entire home.

CLEANING A ROOM— THE RIGHT WAY

Rooms in general

1. Open windows.
2. Empty vases of dead flowers, empty ash trays and waste paper baskets, throw away old newspapers.
3. Put away toys, magazines, books, games, correspondence, etc.

4. Clean out grates and fireplaces if you have open fires or woodburning stoves.

5. Move furniture—out of the room if possible, or at least so you can get behind it.

6. Vacuum curtains, upholstery, and carpets.

7. Mop and polish surrounding areas.

8. Clean windows.

9. Wipe or dust window ledges, wainscotting, polished furniture. Polish where necessary.

10. Shake rugs outside before putting them back.

11. Dust pictures and objects, desks, tables, chairs, shelves, etc.

Bedrooms

1. Put items for washing in laundry basket.

2. Line up boots and shoes to be cleaned.

3. Strip and air the bed.

4. Dust, brush, and vacuum the bedframe and mattress. Turn the mattress. Make the bed.

5. Remove all ornaments and cosmetics from the dressing table and/or bureau; lay them on a cloth on the bed.

6. Dust and polish dressing table and/or bureau.

7. Shake curtains.

Kitchen and bathrooms

Chapter 7 deals exclusively with cleaning these two important rooms.

Cleaning a room—the lazy way

• Generally tidy the room.

• Vacuum and sweep only where it noticeably needs it. Otherwise pick up odd bits of lint and paper with your fingers and leave it at that.

- Dust and wipe surfaces only where they noticeably need it.

- Clean windows only when the glass begins to look smudgy in sunlight.

- Vacuum bedframe and turn the mattress only once every two months.

- It is tempting but not recommended to sweep dust under a rug or piece of furniture—it only leads to more work later on, so it isn't really time-saving in the end.

Cleaning a room—the green way

- Use the minimum amount of detergents and chemicals.

- Don't use aerosol spray polishes or cleaners.

- Don't use aerosol air-fresheners: rather make your own potpourri or hang bunches of dried herbs around the room, keep windows open and upholstery and carpets clean, and don't smoke in the house.

- Use fly paper rather than aerosol or other insecticides.

- Use natural products such as white vinegar, lemon juice, and baking soda instead of toxic and polluting commercial household cleaners, many of which don't even list their ingredients on the package.

- Use detergents with as few additives as possible: no phosphates, perfumes, or enzymes please.

SPRING CLEANING

Theoretically, spring cleaning is a thing of the past, but there's a lot to be said for a good, thorough clear-out once a year. And spring is the best time to do it, when the first sunbeams show up grimy windows and flecks of dust.

This is also a good time to check for repairs and any exterior work that needs doing, such as gutter clearing or the odd roof tile being replaced.

Internal spring cleaning checklist

1. Give each room a thorough going-over as described on pages 71–72, remembering the normally untouched areas such as behind doors, above door frames, under tables and chests of drawers, etc.

2. Clean out closets and ruthlessly throw away "useful" objects you have not used for the past year.

3. Get chimneys swept if you have open fires.

4. Take out books and dust them and the shelves.

5. Sort out and dispose of clothes you never use.

6. Clean upholstery and curtains.

7. Clean carpets and rugs or get them professionally cleaned.

8. Clean out the linen closet. Throw away worn sheets, pillow cases and towels or cut them up to make dust rags.

9. Wash blankets and comforters or have them cleaned.

10. Clean windows downstairs (see page 111). Get a window cleaner to do the upstairs windows.

11. Wash walls and woodwork if you haven't been wiping them clean throughout the year. The woodwork in homes where people smoke nearly always needs a thorough washing.

12. Clear out pantry, kitchen cupboards, and drawers. Throw away any pieces of cracked and broken china as they may harbor germs.

13. Defrost and clean out the freezer (see page 79).

14. Clean or replace the filter on range hood and exhaust fan.

15. Oil metal curtain rods and sliding door tracks.

16. Remove and clean light fixtures.

External spring cleaning checklist

1. Clear out gutters and drain pipes.
2. Check windows for joints and crevices where water might get lodged. Clean down exterior window frames and use a rust primer for rusty patches on metal frames.
3. Check the roof for loose or broken slates or tiles.
4. Check the grouting on outside walls. Damaged pointing allows the walls to absorb water, which will eventually damage the material and allow moisture into the house.

7

Cleaning the Kitchen and Bathroom

The kitchen and the bathroom are the rooms that require the most thorough cleaning because each produces potentially more bacteria than any other room in the house, and because they create warm, steamy atmospheres where those bacteria can thrive. Salmonella scares have reminded us all how important it is to keep the kitchen and everything in it spotlessly clean and germ free.

It is important to keep surfaces in both rooms clean and dry at all times, to rinse cloths and sponges whenever they are used, to dry them quickly and to wash hands after cleaning or before any food preparation.

Chapters 8 and 9 deal with cleaning floors, walls and ceilings. This chapter concentrates on fixtures and items specific to kitchens and bathrooms.

KITCHEN

For maximum efficiency and hygiene, kitchen appliances should be regularly cleaned. Don't allow the dirt to build up—particularly on ovens and stovetops—or the eventual task of cleaning will be far more difficult and unpleasant.

Stove

Gas and electric stovetops
Before cleaning, make sure it is off.

- Don't soak any electrical parts in water.

- After using the stove, allow to cool then take off removable parts. Wash in the sink in hot water and detergent. Wipe over the whole stove and rub stubborn grease spots or burned-on food with a nylon scourer. Don't scrape the surfaces with a knife, even a blunt one.

- Clean really dirty stoves with a commercial oven-cleaning spray applied with an old toothbrush. Leave it on for an hour or two and rinse it off with warm water. Wear gloves to protect your hands.

- For a green way of cleaning the stove, use white vinegar.

Gas and electric ovens
There are various oven-cleaning products available. Some can be used in a cold oven. They are nearly all caustic (most contain lye). If the oven is very dirty, you may have to rub it with steel wool as well.

- Baking soda used on a damp cloth is the green way to clean ovens.

- Self-cleaning ovens or those with detachable non-stick sides should be cleaned according to the manufacturer's instructions. Don't use caustic oven cleaners on them.

- Glass doors can be cleaned with baking soda and a gentle rub with steel wool.

Grill
This should burn itself clean. It can be wiped with liquid detergent solution if necessary.

Microwave ovens

- Wipe the interior with a damp cloth after every use.

- Clean the outside with all-purpose kitchen cleaner.
- The green way is to sit a bowl of hot water with a slice of lemon in it in the oven. Bring to a boil and boil until the interior is good and steamy. Then wipe the interior with a damp cloth.

Exhaust fans and range hoods

Exhaust fans
Switch off fan and unplug.

- Remove outer cover and wash in warm water and detergent.
- Wipe fan blades with a damp cloth. Don't get them wet.
- Dry everything and replace cover.

Range hoods
Clean outside regularly to prevent grease building up.

- Every six months to a year, clean or replace the filter or it may catch fire. Some have a light to indicate when the filter needs replacing. The more frying you do the more often the filter will need attention.

Refrigerator

Refer to the instruction manual for the recommended way of cleaning your refrigerator.

- Wipe up anything spilled in the refrigerator at once.
- Non-automatic refrigerators should be defrosted once a week or once a fortnight or they will run inefficiently.
- The freezer should only need cleaning once a year.
- Even automatically defrosting refrigerators must be cleaned manually from time to time.
- When defrosting, lift out all removable trays, drawers, and shelves. Wash them and the refrigerator interior in warm

detergent and water or wipe with a cloth dipped in baking soda. Don't use anything abrasive.

- Wipe the outside with detergent and water or, for a greener way, with white vinegar and water.
- Switch off the electricity and clean the back of the refrigerator with the brush attachment of the vacuum cleaner.
- Bags filled with carbon (available from hardware stores) will absorb smells in the fridge. So will an open box of baking soda placed inside. Replace every six months or when smells are no longer absorbed.
- If you go away and turn off the electricity, remove all food, wipe out the refrigerator and leave the door open or the whole interior will become moldy.

Freezer

If you keep the door or lid tightly closed, opening and closing it as little as possible, then the freezer should only need defrosting once a year, and that is the time to clean it. Choose a time when stock is low—January and February are usually good months, coming after Christmas but before you've stocked it up with garden produce. In any case, the freezer should be defrosted when frost has built up to ¼ inch.

1. Turn off the electricity and remove any frozen foods.
2. Wrap food in several layers of old newspapers and put a blanket or comforter around it.
3. Make sure any drainage holes are unblocked and place a container or tray under them to collect water.
4. To hasten defrosting, place pans or buckets of hot water in the freezer. Don't use any sharp implement to scrape the ice off in an attempt to speed things up.
5. Mop up water and ice. A large old bath towel will save a lot of cloth-wringing.
6. Wipe the interior with a cloth wrung out in a solution of baking soda and water. Wipe with a dry cloth.

7. Switch on the electricity and put the food back.

8. Wipe the outside of the freezer with warm water and detergent.

Sink

- Clean after each use with an all-purpose liquid cleaner or detergent and water. You may find initial cleaning easier with an angled brush rather than a sponge. Wipe dry.

- Occasionally place a handful of dry washing soda over the drain outlet and pour a pot of hot water over them to keep the S-bend clean and clear.

- From time to time rub the spigots and faucet with half a cut lemon and leave for a few minutes then wipe dry. This gets rid of limescale.

Worktops

Remove everything from the worktop before you begin cleaning it. Food preparation areas should be wiped after every use to prevent the transfer of bacteria from contaminated food (e.g., raw meat) to uncontaminated food.

Laminated tops
Wipe with a damp cloth dipped in baking soda.

Untreated wooden tops
Rub with teak oil or linseed oil.

- Treat heat marks with equal parts of linseed oil and all-purpose cleaning fluid and wipe off. Or try lemon juice or a wood bleach.

Slate worktops
Wipe with a cloth dipped in milk to give a matt luster.

Marble worktops

Wipe regularly with a cloth wrung out in a solution of mild detergent and water. Or wipe it over *quickly* with lemon juice or white vinegar.

* Marble is porous so don't let water or any other liquid sit on it.

Ceramic tops

These just need wiping with a damp cloth or lemon juice.

Kitchen cabinets

Clean out cabinets where food is kept once a month or so. The rest of the cabinets will probably need cleaning out only about once a year.

1. Remove everything from the shelves.
2. Clean inside thoroughly with detergent and water, especially in the corners, making sure you get rid of all crumbs.
3. Leave doors open while surfaces dry.
4. Throw away old opened jars and packages of food.
5. Wipe all jars and bottles with detergent and warm water. Dry, then replace in cabinets.
6. Wash any glasses, dishes, or pots and pans that haven't been used for some time. Replace in cabinets.

Cleaning electrical appliances

Switch off and disconnect all appliances from the outlet before cleaning, and don't put any electrical parts in water.

* Wipe the exteriors of all kitchen machinery frequently with a damp cloth.
* Chrome can be cleaned with a damp cloth dipped in baking soda. Don't use scouring pads or abrasive cleaners.

- Clean all equipment used for preparing food immediately after use.

- Leave the sharp blades and discs of blenders and food processors on the worktop or soaking in a small bowl until you are ready to wash them. Clean them one at a time under running water, using a brush.

- Use a toothbrush to get rid of oily deposits in the base of mixers.

- Turn the toaster upside down and shake out the crumbs.

- Treat kettles with hard water deposits with a commercial descaler (delimer), following the manufacturer's instructions. Or cover the bottom with white vinegar, bring to the boil, allow to cool and pour the vinegar away. Rinse well. Boil up some water and pour that away before using the kettle again.

DISHWASHING BY HAND— THE RIGHT WAY

Dishwashing is everyone's least favorite chore (especially if you don't have a dishwasher), but if you go about it *the right way* it should be relatively painless. See Chapters 12 and 13 for how to clean metal pots, pans, and baking trays.

1. First clear the decks: see that the dish rack is empty and ready for use.

2. Stack up dirty plates and dishes and leave silverware in a bowl or pan of warm water to make it easier to wash. Keep wood, bone, and ivory handles out of the water.

3. Fill the sink or a plastic tub in the sink with hot water and just enough detergent to deal with the grease. The hotter the water, the quicker it will evaporate from items put to drain and the less drying you will have to do.

4. Scrape off uneaten food into the trash and rinse coffee grounds, tea leaves, etc.

5. Wash the cleaner items first, e.g., glasses, and the greasy items last. Wash each piece separately. Lift stemmed glasses by the stem.

6. After washing rinse everything in clean warm water. Don't use cold water or the sudden change in temperature from hot to cold could cause glasses and china to crack.

7. Put silverware directly into a silverware drainer; knives sharp side down. Never leave knives or food processor blades in the dishwater; someone may put their hand in and cut themselves.

8. Stack items carefully in the dish rack and on the draining board.

9. Dry and polish items with a clean, dry towel.

10. Put items away as soon as they are dry.

11. Wipe down the sink and draining board.

Dishwashing by hand—the lazy way

• Soak burned-on food overnight.

• Fit a wall-mounted plate rack above the draining board and store plates in it permanently, putting them there after washing the dishes and without bothering to dry them.

• Allow silverware and dishes to drain dry without using a towel.

• Make those who have not done the cooking wash the dishes.

• Use a dishwasher (see page 84).

Dishwashing by hand—the green way

• Use a plastic tub rather than filling a large sink with water.

• Don't use detergent unless you live in a hard water area,

and then very little. In soft water areas hot water alone should be sufficient for dishwashing.

- Don't rinse items under a hot running tap as it's very wasteful. Instead use a separate bowl or tub of clean water.

- In summer save the bowl or tub of rinsing water to water the garden with.

Using a dishwasher

- Don't use too much detergent, especially in soft water areas or if your machine has a built-in water softener—in which case refill with water softener regularly.

- Load carefully, checking that no items will obstruct the jets of water or the revolving spray arm (if your machine has one). Similarly don't block the detergent dispenser outlet.

- Stack items with their rims facing downward.

- Don't put silver utensils in the same basket as stainless steel.

- Anchor lightweight or unstable items between other items.

- Empty the machine as soon as the drying cycle is completed.

- Don't dishwash thin or heat sensitive plastics, wooden bowls, insulated ware (such as thermoses), glass with metal trim, delicate china or cut glass, ironware, lacquered metals, or high gloss aluminum.

- Avoid running the dishwasher half empty. It's more economical and "greener" to wait until you have a full load.

BATHROOM

Keep the bathroom as clean and dry as you can at all times. The flushing of the toilet produces a fine spray of infected water droplets, whether the lid is closed or not. These will land on doors and walls so regular wiping down of all bathroom surfaces with mild detergent and water is important.

• As well as surfaces, frequently wipe down all bathroom fixtures with a solution of mild detergent and water.

• Wipe sink, bathtub, and/or shower after each use.

• To clean the toilet brush, hold it under the toilet flush before allowing it to drain and putting it back in the holder.

• Keep cleaning equipment in obvious and reachable places.

Cleaning baths and sinks—the right way

• Don't use abrasive cleaners or very strong bathroom cleaners on baths, sinks, or showers.

• Clean vitreous enamel (porcelain) bathtubs and ceramic showers and sinks with foam bathroom cleaner applied on a cloth or soft sponge. Rinse well.

• Clean acrylic or fiberglass tubs with mild detergent solution. Rub stubborn stains with half a lemon. Rub scratches with silver polish. If necessary use diluted household bleach or hydrogen peroxide but don't leave it on. Rinse well.

• Remove hard water marks with a commercial limescale remover.

• Remove rust marks with rust remover or use a paste of cream of tartar and hydrogen peroxide and a drop or two of household ammonia. Leave on for an hour or two before wiping clean. Rinse.

• Regularly remove hair balls from drains.

Cleaning baths and sinks—the lazy way

• Get everyone to wipe out the bath or sink after they've used it.

- Use a bubble bath that cleans the bath at the same time rather than leaving a ring.
- Don't use bath oils.
- Don't allow limescale to build up until it becomes difficult to remove.
- Mineral spirits will usually remove most stubborn greasy stains caused by bath oils, etc.

Cleaning baths and sinks—the green way

Instead of commercial bath-cleaning products use vinegar and water or lemon juice.

- Clean hard water marks with vinegar or lemon juice. For stubborn marks soak cotton wool or paper towels in white vinegar and leave them on for an hour or so before rubbing the marks away.
- Rub rust stains with a paste made of borax and lemon juice.

Cleaning the toilet—the right way

- Rub the inside of the toilet bowl every day with the toilet brush and a toilet bowl cleaner. Remember to clean under the rim. Don't use two different cleaners at the same time—they may combine to produce explosive or toxic gases.
- Wash seat, handle, and surrounding area daily. A very dirty toilet can be emptied of water by pushing the water through with a cloth tied around the toilet brush. When it is empty, use a toilet bowl cleaner in the bowl and leave for an hour or two.

Cleaning the toilet—the lazy way

Use an automatic toilet bowl cleaner, one of those that makes the water blue. Every time the toilet is flushed, some of the cleaner is released. This does NOT eliminate the need to use a toilet brush entirely or the need to wipe the surrounding area daily.

Cleaning the toilet—the green way

• Use white vinegar instead of commercial toilet-bowl cleaners to clean the toilet and surrounding area.

Cleaning other bathroom items

Shower head
Soak in white vinegar or brush with white vinegar on an old toothbrush.

Bathroom cupboard/medicine chest

• Clear out regularly. Dispose of old medicines.
• Wipe out the inside with a clean cloth.

Bidets
Clean with mild disinfectant or white vinegar and wipe dry. Clean the inside overflow with a toothbrush or bottle brush kept specially for the purpose.

Bath towels and mats

• Wash towels and bathmats at least once a week. If bath-mats can't be put in the dryer, hang them over the side of the bath or over a heated towel rail after use so that they can dry out.
• Wash plastic mats in the sink or bathtub in warm water and detergent solution.
• Wipe cork mats with a damp cloth.

Bath sponges and washcloths

• Rinse thoroughly after use and hang up to dry.

- Wash occasionally in weak vinegar solution (¼ cup of white vinegar to a bowl of water) or in the washing machine. Hang to dry.

Shower curtains

- Remove spots of mildew with baking soda on a damp cloth.
- Large areas of mildew should be washed with hot water and detergent and then rubbed with lemon juice. Dry in the sun if possible.
- To machine wash a shower curtain see page 13.

8

Cleaning Floors

If you can keep the floor clean, the rest of the house will look basically OK. This is partly because in order to clean the floor properly, you do need to do some clearing and tidying but also because the floor is the background to everything else and whatever it looks like will affect the appearance of the room. So if guests are arriving in 10 minutes and there isn't time to clean everything, get the vacuum and whiz round for an instant transformation.

Sweeping and vacuuming little but often is a good general rule for floors and carpets, but occasionally they do need something more drastic, like washing and polishing or shampooing.

WASHING A FLOOR—
THE RIGHT WAY

The following method will remove dirt and old polish, but don't use it for wooden floors, which should not get too wet and should just be wiped over with a damp mop. It's best to have two mops for this method and possibly a squeegee—a rubber strip in a holder on the end of a handle, usually used for cleaning windows but excellent for floors too.

1. Move all the furniture out of the room.

- Slip heavy socks over the legs to make moving easier and to prevent the floor from getting scratched.

2. Sweep or vacuum the floor thoroughly.

3. Apply detergent solution with a sponge or wet mop.

4. Leave detergent for a few minutes so that it can get into the dirt. Don't allow it to run under skirting boards where it may saturate electric wires and sockets.

5. Scrub any very dirty marks and in corners. Use a nylon pad or wire wool if necessary.

6. A squeegee is the ideal tool for scraping up muck from very dirty floors.

7. Afterward wipe with a nearly-dry mop. Rinse it frequently while working. Rinsing is important so as not to leave a thin film of detergent, which will prevent any polish from being absorbed and make the floor slippery and dangerous.

Washing a floor—the lazy way

Wipe over with a sponge mop squeezed out in a weak solution of detergent and water. Wipe over again with the same mop squeezed out in clear warm water.

Washing a floor—the green way

- Instead of detergent solution use ¼ cup of white vinegar in a bowl of water. Very dirty patches can be rubbed with straight vinegar. Leave it on for a few minutes before wiping it clean.

- Many floor-cleaning products contain toxic chemicals such as ethanol, formaldehyde, and chlorine, so avoid using them.

POLISHING FLOORS— THE RIGHT WAY

Don't use too much polish. One application a month or less is quite enough; otherwise it will build up into a slippery dirt trap. Just buff up in between from time to time. You can buff up with a piece of waxed paper placed under the mop, which will help to pick up dirt.

There are basically three types of floor polish:

Wax polish
Available as either liquid wax, which is easy to apply and helps to clean the floor, or solid wax polish. Both are suitable for unvarnished wood, linoleum, and cork. Solid wax can be thinned with turpentine, but why not use liquid wax in the first place?

Liquid solvent polish
The solvent evaporates after application, leaving behind the polish. For wood, linoleum and cork, as above. Don't use it on polyurethane or vinyl or anything that the solvent could damage.

Water-based polish (e.g., Mop & Glow)
These types of polish generally have silicones in them. They are easy to apply and long lasting. Use them on any floor except unvarnished or unsealed wood, linoleum, or cork. Be sparing with them because they can build up to become very slippery.

Preparation

Vacuum or sweep up as much grit and dust as you can, then remove any big buildup of old polish so that you can start again from scratch:

1. Mix a bucket of detergent and water with a little ammonia, or, preferably, a bucket of a strong solution of white vinegar and water.

2. Apply with a mop and as soon as dirt and wax begin to dissolve, wipe it all off using a squeegee. Work on a small area at a time, and don't let the cleaner sink right in. If you have no squeegee, crumpled newspaper or a sponge mop will do.

3. Wipe off with a clean mop.

4. Move on to the next area.

5. Let the floor dry thoroughly before you apply new polish.

Applying the polish

1. Apply polish evenly and lightly to a clean, dry floor with a soft cloth. Allow to soak in.

2. Buff up with a broom head tied up in an old terrycloth towel or with a "dumper" (a heavily padded weight on a stick), or use an electric floor polisher. These can be rented or bought. Or you can, of course, get down on your hands and knees and buff up the floor by hand.

3. Don't apply more polish for another two or three months. Just buff up in between.

4. Build up the surface with two or three thin coats rather than applying one enormously thick one. The first coat should cover the whole floor, the next two only the well worn areas.

5. Don't splash walls, etc., with polish as it is difficult to remove.

6. To clean floor polisher pads, place them between several thicknesses of paper towels and press with a warm iron. The towels will absorb the warm wax.

Polishing floors—the lazy way

1. Don't bother to remove old polish but do make sure the floor is clean and vacuum or sweep up as much grit and dust as you can.

2. Apply polish to a dust rag tied around the head of a broom. Rub this over the main traffic areas.

3. Buff up with a clean cloth tied around the broom.

   • Or don't apply more polish at all—simply buff up where necessary.

Polishing—the green way

• Good polishing practice is to be economical with the polish, otherwise the floor may become slippery. This is also the green way. Less polish means fewer silicones, synthetic solvents, and artificial perfumes.

• Do not use aerosol polishes.

SPECIAL TREATMENTS FOR PARTICULAR FLOORS

Certain types of flooring require specialized treatment to maintain their appearance.

Asphalt
Wash occasionally with warm water and mild detergent. Rinse and dry.

• Don't use abrasives or abrasive cleaning powders.

• Don't use old or wax-based polishes. Use a water-based floor polish instead.

• Don't apply too much or the floor will become slippery.

• Don't use solvents, which will soften the surface.

Ceramic tiles
Mop with mild detergent and water.

- Remove spilled nail polish by allowing it to dry and then peeling it off.

Concrete

Don't use soap on unsealed concrete floors. Seal the surface to make it easier to sweep and wash. Or use a wax polish.

Cork

Polish plain cork; wash sealed cork. Vinyl-covered cork tiles can be mopped with mild detergent and water.

- Don't allow cork to get very wet, and dry it thoroughly after washing.

Floor paint

Paints are available which can be applied to vinyl, linoleum, wood, etc. Painted floors are easier to clean if they have a wax polish or have been varnished or sealed, in which case wash them with mild detergent and water.

- Glossy enamel paint can be washed with hot water. Rub gently. Remove stubborn spots with a very mild scouring powder or fine steel wool.

Linoleum

This is a natural material based on linseed oil and finely ground cork. Mop it with warm detergenty water, but don't scrub. Dry the floor thoroughly.

- Remove marks by rubbing with medium-grade steel wool dipped in turpentine.

- Remove crayon marks with a little silver polish.

- Remove grease spills by applying ice cubes immediately then removing congealed grease and washing with detergent and water.

- Polish it or seal it as for wood. If you want to use a sealant, an oil-based one will bond better than a plastic-based one.

Marble
A luxury natural stone that needs very little maintenance. Use diluted dishwashing liquid on a soft mop or cloth and wipe dry immediately. If there is any staining or blistering get professional advice. Don't use abrasives. Marble is porous and oils and fats will stain it while acids will pit it.

Polyurethane
Mop with detergent solution and polish if you want to with a water-based polish. Don't use solvent-based cleaners or polishes as they will soften and damage the tiles.

Quarry tiles
Rub tiles with linseed oil when new and don't wash them at all until two weeks after they have been laid. Damp-mop with warm detergenty water and scrub them if necessary.

- Newly laid tiles may acquire white patches, which are caused by lime in the cement. Wash these in a weak solution of white vinegar and water.

- Use a silicone polish if you want to, but polish is not really necessary.

- Front steps tiled with quarry tiles are sometimes maintained with a red-colored wax polish.

Rubber
This can be protected with a water-based sealer. Wash with detergent and water. Polish with a special rubber polish or water-based polish. Polishes based on waxes or solvents will dissolve rubber.

Slate
Wash or scrub with a solution of washing soda and detergent. Apply a little lemon juice or milk after washing to give a lustrous finish. Remove all excess with a clean cloth.

Stairs
Start from the bottom and work up.

Stone
Stone floors are porous. Mop or scrub with washing soda or detergent solution.

• Protect stone floors with a cement sealer and wax-polish thereafter.

Terrazzo
A mixture of marble chips set in cement. Mop with a solution of dishwashing liquid and water. Don't get terrazzo too wet. Dry well immediately after washing. Don't use steel wool or abrasive powders.

Varnish
Mop with detergent solution. No need to polish.

Vinyl
Mop with detergent solution. Polish, if you want to, with a water-based polish. Don't use solvent-based cleaners or polishes as they will soften and damage the tiles.

• Remove crayon marks with silver polish.

• Remove grease spills by applying ice cubes immediately. When congealed, scrape up grease and clean with detergent solution.

Wood
Mop sanded and sealed floors with warm, not hot, water and detergent. Don't allow the floor to get too wet. When the seal begins to wear off, reseal it.

• Don't wash polished wood floors but after some years, when the polish has built up, you can wipe it with a cloth dipped in white vinegar and water to remove excess polish and dirt. Apply new polish sparingly and infrequently. Buff up in between. Liquid wax polish helps to remove dirt and is easier to apply than solid wax.

• If grease gets spilled, apply ice cubes immediately and

then scrape the grease up and clean with detergent and water.

- Oil and grease stains can be removed with a paste of fuller's earth and soap and water. Put it on the stain and leave for two or three days to draw out the mark.

- A paste wax will also help to remove tar spots.

- Remove spilled nail polish from waxed and shiny floors by allowing it to dry and then peeling it off. If you try and wipe it up while it is still wet you will leave smears.

CLEANING CARPETS AND SOFT FLOORCOVERINGS

On the whole we treat our carpets extraordinarily badly. We walk on them in heavy and high heeled shoes, tread mud into them, spill things on them and still expect them to last forever. If a carpet is to last it must be kept clean on a regular basis. Dust and grit are more damaging to carpets than other types of flooring since they split and cut the fibers when anyone walks over them. Anything spilled should be swept or absorbed at once.

- Occasionally (and BEFORE it actually looks grubby) give your carpet a good shampoo.

Vacuuming—the right way

The original upright vacuum cleaner that beats-as-it-sweeps-as-it-cleans is still probably the most satisfactory type for a fully carpeted home. But cylinder cleaners are more convenient for homes with a mixture of smooth floors and carpet and take up less storage space in a small home. Get one with a powerful motor, since there is no beating action to bring grit to the surface.

1. Pick up by hand all sharp, hard and ungainly objects such as nails, buttons, etc. as they can damage the machine.
2. Move all the furniture off the carpet.
3. Run the cleaner over each area of carpet at least 12 times, overlapping each stroke.
4. If the carpet is loose, vacuum underneath first, and then on top.

Vacuuming—the lazy way

- Just move small pieces of furniture and objects off the floor.
- Vacuum an area until it looks respectable—don't bother with 12 strokes.

Vacuuming—the green way

- Don't use perfumed vacuuming powders.
- Reuse dust bags a couple of times before throwing away.

Shampooing carpets—the right way

Check with the manufacturer before attempting to shampoo a carpet as some carpets should only be dry-cleaned. If in doubt call a professional cleaner.

1. Remove all furniture from the room.
2. Vacuum thoroughly (see page 97).
3. Test a small piece of carpet for colorfastness (see page 5). Acetic acid or vinegar added to the shampoo may prevent the color from running.
4. Follow the instructions on the carpet shampoo package. Use only lukewarm water. Apply gently with a soft bristle brush and don't brush synthetics too hard without enough shampoo to lubricate them or the fibers may crack or be-

come frizzy. Treat very dirty areas twice or the end result may be patchy.

5. Vacuum again to remove dry foam and dirt and to raise the pile. Vacuum again the following day.

6. Allow the carpet to dry completely before putting the furniture back. Or put a piece of greaseproof paper or aluminum foil or special plastic stands under furniture legs and castors to prevent rust stains. Don't walk on carpet while it is damp. Put brown paper, a plastic tarp, or shelf paper down.

7. Brush the carpet all over in the direction of the pile. This is particularly important on cotton carpets as the pile is liable to flatten easily.

General carpet-shampooing advice

• Treat stains before shampooing the carpet (see Chapters 3 and 4 and page 101).

• Be sure to use a carpet shampoo not just any old detergent that may contain bleach and alkalis and would be damaging to carpets.

• A 220-pound wool carpet will absorb about 35 pounds of water before the backing becomes saturated, but a 220-pound synthetic carpet may absorb only about 6 pounds of water before the backing is affected, so take special care not to get synthetic carpets very wet.

• Cotton takes a long time to dry out, so there's more chance of mildew forming and of the color running on cotton carpets. Dry foam shampoos are useful for these.

• If the carpet gets overly wet, fold a thick towel, place it over the wet area and stand on it. Don't rub. Wet carpets can also be suspended on bricks to allow air to circulate underneath.

• Synthetics may attract static. Use an anti-static product that will last for about 12 months. Or sprinkle the carpet very lightly with water from a fine spray nozzle because lack of moisture is the main cause of static.

Shampooing carpets—the lazy way

- Hire a professional carpet cleaner to clean the carpets for you. Look in the Yellow Pages for the name of a local cleaner. If you're having a carpet professionally cleaned, find out first whether the price includes moving the furniture. Some companies offer a discount if they don't have to do this. Some cleaners offer "chemical" cleaning, but this is rather drastic and not to be recommended.

- Alternatively rent a carpet-cleaning machine. This is worthwhile particularly if you are cleaning a lot of carpets or the carpet is very dirty. Use the machine with the recommended shampoo.

- Have a new or newly cleaned carpet treated with silicone (or use a sealer such as Scotchguard) to prevent the carpet getting dirty again too quickly and to make future cleaning easier. Treatments should last for about three years.

Shampooing carpets—the green way

- Use the minimum amount of detergent or use a dry shampoo.
- Don't use aerosols.

CARE OF OTHER SOFT FLOORINGS

Carpet tiles
Can be lifted individually if anything gets spilled on them. If irretrievably stained, swap with unseen tile (e.g., one behind a door) or replace with a new one. It is useful to buy a few extra that can be slotted in if necessary.

Small cotton rugs
Machine wash.

Fur rugs

If on a felt, wool, or flannel backing, clean with fuller's earth or talcum powder: shake it over the rug and leave it for several hours, then brush and shake it out.

- Wipe non-backed rugs with a cloth wrung out in lukewarm water and mild detergent.

Hooked rugs

Vacuum and sweep, but don't beat or shake in case the loops become loose. Any further cleaning should be done by a professional.

Numdah rugs (embroidered Indian matted goat's hair)

Dry-clean only. Vacuum, but not with a cleaner that beats.

Doormat, coconut, sisal, rush matting

Lift and shake out of doors and vacuum up the enormous quantity of dust that will have collected underneath. Some mats now have an impermeable backing that makes cleaning easier. If the matting is not movable, vacuum as often as you can.

STAIN REMOVAL GUIDELINES

Follow the guidelines on pages 34–59, remembering the following points:

- The secret of successful stain removal is speed—the sooner you catch the stain the better.

- Don't get the carpet too wet.

- Blot well between applications of cleaning fluid: terry-cloth toweling will absorb a good deal of moisture. Tread it into the carpet to reach the wet fibers at the bottom.

- Do not rub or brush a carpet too vigorously when cleaning.

- Remove stains before shampooing the carpet.

- Test for colorfastness before applying solvent cleaners.

- Grease, oil, and tar can be cleaned with dry-cleaning solvent in a circular motion, working from the edge of the stain to the center. Allow to dry then follow with detergent and water, blotting between applications. Rinse well, blotting as before. Dry with a clean towel.

- Urine, feces, and vomit can be scraped up with a blunt knife. Then sponge with mixed up carpet shampoo, adding ¼ cup white vinegar to each pint, or use a commercial spotting kit.

- Don't use detergents if you don't know what was spilled. If you do use detergent, dishwashing liquid is probably as good as any.

- Certain spot removers that can safely be used on wool (i.e., nail-polish remover and acetone) may destroy certain acetates.

- Use acids (e.g., white vinegar) to remove stains from wool, camel hair, mohair, and other organic or protein fibers and polyester.

- Use alkalis (e.g., baking soda or a weak solution of household ammonia) on cellulose or vegetable fibers such as cotton, jute, viscose and rayon, silk and nylon.

9

Cleaning Walls and Ceilings

The main difficulty with cleaning walls and ceilings is their height. Make sure you have a set of sturdy steps, some absorbent cloths or sponges, a bucket of warm detergenty water, and another bucket of clean rinsing water. If possible put the buckets on a chair, table, or stool next to where you are working so you can reach them from your work station. The best cloths are clean cotton cloths or old terry cloth towels rather than disposable cloths, which are generally not absorbent enough.

When cleaning walls near the stairs, lean a ladder against the wall with its base supported by the angle of the stair. Place a stepladder on the landing and a wide plank on one rung of the steps and one rung of the ladder.

WASHING PAINTWORK— THE RIGHT WAY

Walls
For very dirty walls, or before repainting, use a solution of mild detergent and water.

1. Squeeze out a sponge or cloth in the detergent solution. You need just enough to get at the dirt, not enough to run down the wall (or your shirtsleeve) in streaks.

2. Start at the top and work down. Work on one reachable section at a time. Sponge or wipe the area with detergent.

3. When you have covered a section, go back to the beginning with a clean cloth wrung out in clean water and wipe off detergent and dirt.

   • If the walls are very dirty, allow the detergent a little longer to work on the dirt before wiping it off.

   • Change the water in the bucket frequently.

   • On gloss walls, give a final wipe with a clean, dry towel to remove any detergent streaks on the paint.

Ceilings

If the ceiling has yellowed with smoke, age, water stains, fluorescent tube marks, etc., slap a coat of water-based paint on. This is easier and more effective than trying to wash the ceiling. If you must clean it, use a clean, dry broom rather than a wet cloth or sponge. Take down light fixtures and clean them at the same time.

• Acoustic tile ceilings can be cleaned with a dry sponge once a year.

• Cover small marks on white ceilings with a dab of white shoe polish.

• If you must wash a ceiling, work on 3-foot square sections at a time using the same method given for walls. Cover the floor with a plastic tarp to catch splatters of detergent solution. Wear goggles.

Washing paintwork—the lazy way

• Use a clean sponge floor mop to reach the top of the wall instead of setting up a ladder.

• If you were thinking of it, don't clean the insides of wardrobes and cupboards. When clearing out at spring cleaning time, give them a brush with a clean broom, otherwise leave them alone.

- If your walls are fairly clean, forget about the two buckets mentioned above and just wipe the walls over with a cloth wrung out in warm water with a little white vinegar added.

Washing paintwork—the green way

- Use a weaker solution of detergent with a little white vinegar added or use just water and vinegar.

CLEANING WALLCOVERINGS

Brick

- Brush and vacuum and pull out all loose grit.
- Untreated bricks are best left to acquire a natural patina of grime, and washing them will usually make any marks worse.
- Sealed bricks can be washed with detergent and water.

Ceramic tiles and gloss paints

1. Wipe with a cloth wrung out in detergent (make sure it's soap-free). A sponge mop works well on tiled walls, and a squeegee is also useful for very dirty walls.
2. Wipe with a clean sponge squeezed in clean water.
3. Remove stains with all-purpose cleaner or a nylon pad.

- Car wax is a good tile cleanser and polish. Rub it in with a soft cloth, leave for 10 minutes, but don't allow it to dry completely. Polish with a soft cloth.
- Discolored grout should be rubbed with a toothbrush and commercial bathroom cleaner or half and half solution of household chlorine bleach or liquid antiseptic and water. It

may be easier to re-grout, though, or paint with special grout paint (available in a range of colors).

- For a green way to clean ceramic tiles, rub with a cut lemon. Leave for 15 minutes, then polish with a soft, dry cloth.

Embossed wallpapers

A soft toothbrush will get dust out of valleys.

Fabric and cork

- Dust or vacuum with the dusting attachment of your vacuum cleaner.

- Pat with a damp cloth wrung out in warm water. Test a small patch first to check that the colors won't run.

- Felt should be given a "dry shampoo." Spread bran, fuller's earth, or talcum powder on to the wall. Leave for a few hours and then vacuum. Cover the floor with a ground cloth or plastic tarp because you are bound to spill a good deal. Test a small piece first. Vacuuming may pull the felt from the wall, so you might have to pat it to release the powder instead.

- Cork can be sealed with a matt seal and washed as for washable wallcoverings. If it is not sealed, don't try to wash it, just keep it well dusted.

Lacquered wallpapers

Use warm water and detergent and wash as for walls.

Moldings

- Check that moldings are, indeed, washable and that any chips and cracks won't be further damaged by the water. Don't wash plaster moldings, which will smudge and streak. Paint them instead, when you next paint the ceiling.

- Dust with a cobweb brush or a feather duster on a long handle.

- If moldings are very dirty, spray with detergent and water in a spray bottle with a fine spray. Wait for the liquid to penetrate then wipe with a dry cloth and spray again with clear water.

- Terrycloth towels are good for moldings because the loops of thread mop up water in the crevices.

Non-washable wallcoverings

- Brush occasionally with a cobweb brush or broom.

- Pat stubborn marks lightly with a damp cloth. Gently pat the paper dry. Don't rub.

- Cleaners are available of modeling-dough texture, which can be used to gently erase stains. Or use a soft eraser or lumps of bread. Use them with a downward sweeping movement. Don't press too hard and don't rub sideways. None of these will remove marks on very dirty walls or get rid of crayon marks and they may themselves leave streaky marks.

Washable papers

These are not really "washable" but can be sponged gently with mild soapflakes and water applied on a soft sponge and patted dry with a clean cloth.

Washable wallcoverings (textured vinyl, etc.)

- Dust frequently because dirt tends to make the wallcovering brittle.

- If necessary wipe with detergent and water on a cloth or sponge. You can use dry-cleaning solvents on stains. Don't use lacquer solvents, which will damage the surface.

Wood paneling

- Waxed or sealed panels just need dusting and the occasional wipe with a sponge wrung out in liquid detergent and water.

- Varnished or lacquered wood should be cleaned with furniture polish.

- Painted panels can be cleaned with detergent and water on a soft cloth or sponge. Don't use abrasive cleaners, steel wool, etc.

- Touch up discolored paneling with shoe polish, dark wax polish, or wood stain. BE CAREFUL. If you make it too dark you can't then lighten it again.

Removing specific stains

If the method of stain removal is going to do a lot of damage to the wall covering, it may be best to live with a mark until you next redecorate.

Ballpoint pen

- On paint use denatured alcohol. You can try this on wallcoverings as well, but don't rub too hard for fear of damaging the finish.

- On walls, try using a soft nail brush or old toothbrush.

- On cork you can try the method above, but it may not work.

- On wood paneling, try a mild detergent solution followed by denatured spirits on cotton wool. But almost any treatment will discolor the wood so you may have to use shoe polish or wood stain to bring it back to its correct color.

- On brick or new plaster, use paint remover and give it time to work on the marks before you scrape it off. Wash with detergent and water. If necessary use fine grade sandpaper.

Crayon

- On paintwork try a dough ball or an eraser (see page 107).

- On most wallcoverings draw out the wax with a warm iron over blotting paper or paper towels, which will absorb it. Any residual stain may be rubbed with mineral spirits or moistened baking soda on a damp cloth.

- On brick, use paint remover and give it time to work on the marks before you scrape it off. Wash with detergent and water. If necessary, use sandpaper.

Fingermarks

These may respond to a little diluted dishwashing liquid rubbed gently in and then rinsed off thoroughly. Rub the mark only and not the surrounding area.

Grease

- On paint, rub with strong detergent and water with a little mineral spirits added.

- On washable and unwashable wallcoverings, draw out the grease with blotting paper or paper towels under a warm iron. Or apply a paste of fuller's earth and dry-cleaning fluid, allow it to dry and then brush it off.

- On embossed wallcoverings, dab with talcum powder, leave for a couple of hours, then brush off gently.

- On vinyl, dab with dry-cleaning solvent and then detergent and water, followed by clean water.

- On cork, dab with water containing borax or a solution of mild detergent and water with a few drops of household ammonia.

- On silk, get professional advice.

- On wood paneling, use a mild detergent and water followed by mineral spirits on cotton wool.

- On brick, sponge with mineral spirits.

Sticky tape

- Masking tape, Scotch tape, and other adhesive tapes should be peeled off while still fresh. If it has been on for some time, it can be difficult to remove. Peel off carefully so you don't leave part of the tape on the wall or tear the wallcovering. Use acetone or non-oily nail-polish remover to soften the glue base. Acetone and nail-polish remover will damage some paints and some plastic surfaces so don't leave them on too long.

- Remove tape by lifting the top edge and pulling it back on itself, keeping it parallel with the wall and pulling slowly and evenly. It may help to use a hair dryer along it, allowing the warmth to soften the glue.

- Old collages or decals may come off if you paint them with several coats of white vinegar. Give it time to soak in and then wash the pictures off. Or let a few drops of oil soak into the stuck paper. Rub gently with a soft cloth.

10

Cleaning Windows and Plate Glass

The difference between looking through clean and dirty windows is amazing. Clean and polish them inside and out and you'll wonder why you didn't do it sooner. House plants will benefit too.

Cleaning windows can be an irritating chore, however, especially if water drips down your arms or the smears just won't come off. Most people tend to use too much detergent in the water when cleaning windows, which results in streaks. One capful of detergent in a bucket of warm water is enough. Many professionals insist that they use just cool, clean water, which is fine for moderately clean windows. But these are just two of the many ways you can clean windows.

CLEANING WINDOWS— THE RIGHT WAY

Equipment

1. You will need ONE of the following:
   - a commercial window cleaning product, such as Windex.
   - a bucket of weak detergent solution (see above).

- between 1 teaspoon and ¼ cup of vinegar in a bucket of warm water.

- simply a bucket of tepid, not hot, water.

- a mixture of equal parts of denatured alcohol, paraffin, and water. Put into a bottle and shake hard and often.

- a mixture of ½ cup ammonia, 1 cup white vinegar, and 2 tablespoons cornstarch in a bucket of tepid water.

2. Bucket of clean, warm water, to rinse the cloth in from time to time.

- On cold days add ½ cup of mineral spirits to each 2 pints of water to prevent it from freezing on the glass— although it's not advisable to wash windows when it is this cold.

3. Squeegee (a rubber strip in a holder on the end of a handle) to clean the window.

4. Lint-free cloths to apply the solution and to wipe the squeegee with.

5. Chamois, scrim, or newspaper to buff up the glass after washing and give a good shine.

6. A sturdy stepladder, not just a chair.

Tips for success

- Clean windows when the sun is NOT shining on them.

- Don't clean windows on a frosty day when the glass is more brittle and may break.

- Clean windows often so that cleaning is easy. Don't let them get really dirty, which will result in a waste of your time and effort.

- Change the water frequently.

- Use all detergents, etc., sparingly or they will cause streaks.

- Use crossways strokes for inside, vertical strokes for outside so that you can see which side the smears are on.

- Commercial window cleaners are for use on dry windows.

Don't use them on windows covered in condensation droplets or on windows you have already made wet with a water or detergent solution.

• Don't use a dry cloth on a dirty window or you'll scratch the glass.

Large windows

1. Take down blinds, curtains, and all objects on the window sill.

2. Clean frames around windows before starting on the glass.

3. Wipe the top of the window with a cloth squeezed out in cleaning mixture.

4. Use a squeegee to wipe across the top of the window, bringing the edge down so that you get right into the corners and sides of the glass.

5. Wipe the squeegee blade on the cloth after each stroke.

6. When you have squeegeed the wet part of the window, continue wiping with the cloth and then the squeegee until you reach the bottom.

7. Wipe the cleaned window with scrim, a chamois, or crumpled newspapers to give it a final shine. If you have such a thing, use a blackboard eraser for extra shine.

Small window panes

1. Take down blinds, curtains, and all objects on the window sill.

2. Clean window frames with detergent and water, before starting on the glass.

3. If using commercial cleaner, follow the instructions. If you are using a homemade mixture, squeeze out the cloth in the bucket of mixture, wringing it out well.

4. Work round the edges of each pane and into the middle.

5. Wipe with a clean cloth squeezed out in the clean water immediately. Don't wait for it to dry.

- Small panes in a glazed bookcase should be dusted and wiped with a very little denatured alcohol or mineral spirits on cotton wool. Use a circular motion. Change the cotton wool as soon as it is dirty.

Cleaning windows—the lazy way

- Leave out the final buff with the scrim, chamois, or newspaper.
- Small panes can usually be left for longer between washes as they don't show the dirt as much as large ones.
- Don't become obsessive about small marks left on the glass when you've finished cleaning. You won't get rid of them by wiping at them individually and they won't show to anyone else. This is the sensible way, not just the lazy way.

Cleaning windows—the green way

- Don't use aerosols of any kind.
- Use any commercial window cleaners and detergents *very* sparingly.
- For preference, use the vinegar and water mixture.
- Fly spots can be removed with cold tea.

GENERAL WINDOW
CLEANING ADVICE

- Don't try to clean windows that are difficult to reach or above first floor level.

- Don't hold the bucket while cleaning, and don't perch it on a window ledge.

- It can be useful to have a squeegee with an extended angle handle.

- Don't waste money on gimmicky window cleaners, such as magnetic ones, which don't really work.

- Remove fresh paint marks with turpentine, dry-cleaning solvent or nail-polish remover on a lint-free cloth.

- Soften dried paint splotches with turpentine or mineral spirits.

- Remove putty marks with ammonia or soften them with turpentine or mineral spirits.

- Don't use any abrasives to clean window glass.

- For very dirty windows add a small amount of dishwashing liquid or borax to the cleaner.

- Remove sticky labels or their adhesive with denatured alcohol or mineral spirits on cotton wool.

- Remove screens before cleaning the windows and brush them with the vacuum cleaner attachment or with a stiff bristle brush.

Other types of glass

Glass shower doors
Get rid of soap and water marks by rubbing with a sponge dipped in white vinegar.

Glass table tops
Clean as for small panes, or try with a squeegee. Use white vinegar and water, or lemon juice, or mineral spirits, or any of the mixtures for window cleaning (see page 111).

- Rub fingermarks on clean glass with a cloth dipped in straight vinegar.

- Remove sticky label or tape marks by rubbing with a little peanut butter then wiping off.

Mirrors
Clean with a soft cloth just dampened with any of the mixtures suggested for window cleaning. Take care not to get water between the mirror and frame or into the backing. The cloth should only be damp, not wet. Finish off with a clean chamois or lint-free cloth.

Painted glass
Don't wash painted glass. Dust it with a very soft paintbrush instead.

Sliding glass doors
Wrap a small cloth around an eraser to get rid of track marks on the glass.

Stained-glass panes
Modern stained glass is usually quite robust. Clean it as for small window panes.

* Antique panes should be washed very gently. Don't use commercial products or detergent.

Cleaning Furniture and Upholstery

Little and often is the best advice for cleaning furniture and upholstery. Dusting and vacuuming and the immediate removal of anything spilled are the things that will do most to give your furniture a longer life and a fresher appearance. When using cleaners and polishes be very sparing, and when vacuuming be very gentle, especially on upholstery fabrics.

WOODEN FURNITURE

All polished, waxed, and untreated woods need regular cleaning to keep them in good condition. The right way, the lazy way, and the green way to treat wood are the same if you avoid aerosol sprays and use only natural furniture polishes like beeswax.

Dusting

Dust polished furniture frequently. Regular and thorough dusting is the most important treatment for good wooden furniture. Take care to remove the dust and not just move it about. Use a clean duster and shake it outside afterward. Don't forget to dust all around the legs, dowels, and feet.

• Don't use a feather duster on valuable furniture because broken feathers can scratch the surface.

Polishing

Polish does not actually penetrate or feed the wood. It protects the surface and gives it an attractive finish. The resulting shine also makes it easier to dust. So when applying any sort of polish it is important to make the coating as thin as possible to show up the wood grain and to prevent a build-up of wax, which will attract dust.

1. Before polishing, you can remove any buildup of old polish with white vinegar on a damp cloth.
2. Greasy marks can be removed with a chamois wrung out in a mixture of 1 tablespoon vinegar in ½ pint of water.
3. Apply polish sparingly on a soft cloth and polish right away with a clean cloth.

• Don't use modern furniture cream polishes on antique pieces because these products contain an emulsifying agent that may harm the wood.
• Synthetic furniture polishes are based on silicones, which are not an environmental hazard in themselves but the synthetic solvents and perfumes that they contain often are.
• Don't use aerosols; apart from the environmental reasons, the solvent comes out with such force that it can damage the polished surface. Where such polishes have been used a lot, the furniture aquires a milky look for which there is no cure.

Wax-polished furniture

This is created by scrubbing the wood with a mixture of wax, turpentine, and coloring, then painstakingly polishing it. The result is a very rich, deep shine.

- Dust. Don't use oiled or treated dusters. Use a clean duster and uncolored polish.
- Remove sticky marks with a cloth wrung out in warm detergent solution or with a cloth dipped in white vinegar.
- Oak and mahogany may be rubbed with a cloth dipped in warm beer.

Untreated wood

Untreated solid wood is sometimes used for kitchen worktops. Oak, maple, and mahogany are popular. There are also untreated teak and pine tables for kitchens.

1. Wipe over the surface with a cloth dipped in white vinegar to remove surface dirt but don't leave the surface wet.
2. Apply a thin coating of teak oil or linseed oil to hardwood tops using a cloth and rubbing along the grain. This will prevent the wood from drying out and protect it from dampness, stains, etc. Do this only about once every six months. Teak and linseed oil are flammable so work away from open flames and throw away the cloth after use.

- Scrub pine tables with a clean scrubbing brush and detergent and water.

Some special cases

Cane, wicker, rattan, and bamboo furniture
This should be brushed and vacuumed regularly as dust collects in the weave.

- Scrub with a solution of salt and water if necessary, then rinse well. Don't use detergent. Dry in the sun if possible.
- Polish with furniture cream polish if necessary.

Carved wood

- Dust with a dry decorator's dusting brush, a watercolor brush or an oil-paint brush.
- Get into crevices with a soft toothbrush. This is also useful for removing polish that has lodged in there.

Gilded finishes
The wood is treated to give the impression of gold.

- Don't let water anywhere near gilding.
- Dust gently using a dry watercolor paintbrush. Don't rub.
- Clean with a soft cloth lightly dipped in warm turpentine or mineral spirits. (Because these spirits are flammable, warm them by standing the bottle in a bowl of hot water rather than letting them anywhere near an open flame or direct heat.)
- Remove stains by gently dabbing with half a raw onion.
- If any piece of gilt seems to be flaking off, get professional advice.
- Don't try to retouch any true gilding yourself. Never be tempted to touch up with gold paint as it is a completely different color and will give a different effect.

Lacquered or Japanese lacquered furniture
Keep in a dry balanced temperature as it will suffer in temperature changes and damp atmospheres.

- Wipe down with a damp cloth.
- Remove fingermarks with a damp chamois leather and buff up gently with a soft duster.
- Occasionally polish surfaces with wax polish.

Polyurethane finish
A tough finish.

- Just wipe over with a damp cloth.

Veneered wood and marquetry
Treat carefully to avoid damaging delicate inlay.

- Dust very carefully using a duster with no frayed edges or loose threads that could catch in the inlays and leave tufts behind or even pull pieces of veneer away.
- Polish with a little furniture cream polish or wax polish depending on the type of wood and finish.
- Mop up water spills immediately, and don't allow the wood to get wet with any cleaning solution.
- Don't polish pieces of wood that are damaged or lifting; if wax gets under them, it will then be impossible to glue them back into place should you ever have the item repaired.
- While cleaning, check the surfaces for any bubbling or damage.

Wooden garden furniture
This is usually made of cedar or other hardwoods. The wood is designed to weather and looks best when it has weathered a bit.

- Wipe with a chamois or cloth wrung out in warm water. Rinse with cold water and dry.
- Remove stains by rubbing gently with fine wire wool along the grain. Don't use abrasives or scrub as though you were dealing with a kitchen table.

Remedial treatments for waxed and polished furniture

Don't treat valuable furniture yourself, get a professional.

Black water marks
Rub the surface with fine steel wool then recolor and repolish.

- Or bleach with a commercial wood bleach.

Cigarette burns
Treat as for white rings (see below).

- If necessary lightly sandpaper the area and build it up again with colored beeswax. Do not do this on valuable antiques.

Dents
Fill small dents by melting equal parts of beeswax and rosin in a double saucepan. While still pliable fill the hole with the mixture and when dry, smooth with fine sandpaper, taking care not to damage the rest of the wood.

Ink stains
Try a commercial wood bleach.

Scratches
Conceal light scratches by rubbing them with the kernel of a walnut or a Brazil nut. This works with lightning speed.

- Or rub them with a commercial scratch cover or furniture polish, working in the direction of the grain.

- Or pour on cod liver oil and leave to soak in.

White frosting
This can sometimes be caused by a damp environment. It may cover the whole surface but probably won't penetrate the wood.

- Dip a piece of fine steel wool into cooking oil and rub along the grain. Finish with a wax polish.

White rings
These may be caused by water or heat.

- Rub gently with a paste of salt and cooking oil on a soft cloth. Polish with a soft, dry cloth.

- Or rub with very fine steel wool and olive oil in the direction of the grain.

- Or apply a paste of mayonnaise, or olive oil, and cigarette ash. Leave for a while, then remove the paste and buff up with a damp cloth.

- Or rub with metal polish along the grain. Buff up with a soft cloth.

LAMINATED PLASTIC FURNITURE

Clean carefully as it is easily scratched.

- Wipe laminated furniture with a cloth wrung out in mild detergent and water. Don't use abrasives, chemical cleaners, or ammonia.

- Rub light stains with a damp cloth dipped in baking soda.

- Rub stubborn stains with non-gel toothpaste or cover them in a paste of baking soda and water and leave for several hours. Then rub briskly before wiping off.

Acrylic furniture
Wipe with a mild detergent and water.

- Rub scratches with metal polish.

CLEANING UPHOLSTERY—
THE RIGHT WAY

As with all fabrics, the more regularly you clean upholstery, the easier it will be. Accumulations of surface dirt, dust, perspiration, hair oil, and so on will damage the fibers—and so will the rigorous cleaning you have to give to really grubby textiles.

General rules

- Vacuum cushions, arm rests, backs, and crevices every week.

- Pat upholstery gently with a plastic fly-swatter or old fashioned carpet beater to loosen the dust before vacuuming.

- Mop up at once anything spilled, before it stains the fabric. Many things are quite easy to get rid of at the time, but impossible later on. Treat according to the stain and type of fabric. See Chapters 3 and 4.

- Turn cushions occasionally so that they wear evenly. Shampoo chairs and seats two or three times a year.

- Don't vacuum fringes or embroidery or anything with beads or sequins on it.

- Don't use a vacuum with extra strong suction. A small, hand-held vacuum is the best type for cleaning upholstery.

- Don't use the brush attachments when vacuuming.

Shampooing upholstery

1. Remove as much surface dirt as possible with a thorough vacuuming, getting into all corners and crevices and working on the seams and piping etc.

2. Spot clean stains at this stage if you didn't do it at the time they were made (see Chapters 3 and 4).

3. Choose a cleaning product suitable for the upholstery fabric. Otherwise, your usual carpet shampoo may be suitable, but use just the foam so as not to get the upholstery too wet.

4. Whatever product you are using, follow the manufacturer's instructions. Test the fabric for colorfastness in an inconspicuous area. Treat it with a little of the upholstery shampoo, leave it for a short while, and then dab it with paper towels. If no color comes off onto the towel, go ahead with the shampooing. If color does come off, either

shampoo with great care or get the piece professionally cleaned.

5. Treat a small area at a time, using as little water and cleaning fluid as possible, so the padding doesn't get wet.

6. For tough fabrics, rub the entire surface vigorously with a damp (not wet) towel to take off the foam residue and loosened dirt. A Turkish towel, which is both rough and absorbent, is excellent. Don't rub delicate fabrics. Blot them instead with clean white paper towels.

7. Blot with tepid water to rinse. Dry with a Turkish towel and don't get the fabric too wet.

8. Allow to dry, then vacuum thoroughly again.

• If, after shampooing, there are still stains, treat with dry-cleaning solvent.

Cleaning upholstery—the lazy way

Dry foam upholstery shampoos are the easiest to use as they dry to form crystals, drawing out the dirt as they dry. The crystals are then vacuumed away. Rub obstinate stains with the applicator brush or a soft toothbrush. Don't brush delicate fabrics. Use a sponge instead.

• Or have the upholstery professionally cleaned.

• Have new or newly cleaned upholstery treated with a stain guard process to prevent it from soiling too quickly.

• Arm caps and head rest covers will protect the areas most quickly soiled.

• Or use removable stretch covers. It is easier to remove these and wash them than to shampoo the upholstery on the furniture.

Cleaning upholstery—the green way

• Avoid aerosol shampoos and stain removers.

- Use the minimum amount of cleaner and don't mix more than you need.

- After shampooing treat any residual stains with a solution of detergent and water, containing 1 teaspoon of white vinegar.

Some special cases

Cushions
These can have removable or non-removable covers.

- Take off and wash removable cushion covers fairly frequently.

- If using upholstery shampoo or dry-cleaning fluids on non-removable covers don't get the fillings too wet.

- Don't wash feather-filled cushions or the feathers will poke out of the fabric.

- Don't wash kapok as it will get lumpy.

Leather upholstery
Dust or vacuum regularly.

- Clean dirty areas with saddle soap, using as little water as possible. When dry, buff up with a soft cloth.

- Rub dark leather every six months or so with castor oil or neat's foot oil to prevent the leather from cracking. Clean the leather first. Apply a small amount of oil with a cottonball or a piece of cotton wool or the fingertips. Rub it in well and take off any surplus.

- Rub pale leather with petroleum jelly.

- Don't wax leather furniture as it won't absorb the wax. You can use a little shoe cream instead if you wish, but make sure you rub it in well and polish off any excess so that it doesn't get transferred to your clothes.

- Sometimes hide begins to get a dried-out look, especially in centrally heated homes. Apply a leather conditioning product with cotton balls. Leave for 24 hours for the leather to absorb it, then buff up with a soft, clean duster.

- Or sponge with vinegar and water with a little ammonia added. While still wet apply castor oil on a rag. When the leather is dry polish with furniture cream.

- When using any sort of leather conditioner be careful not to touch any embossed gilding and keep the product away from any surrounding wood.

Loose covers

- Wash stretch covers at home in the machine.

- Larger cotton and linen covers may be too cumbersome for your washing machine and are difficult to dry at home anyway, so take them to the Laundromat or send to the dry-cleaners.

- Iron on the wrong side so the fabric doesn't get shiny. However, loose covers are difficult to iron because they are so ungainly and bulky. This is another good reason for sending them to the cleaners.

Plastic and vinyl

Use a vinyl cleaner/conditioner to clean vinyl upholstery.

- Wipe sticky marks with a mild soap and water solution. Don't use detergent.

Tapestry and embroidery

Valuable needlepoint or worn tapestry should be dealt with by experts.

- Vacuum needlepoint once a week using low suction and don't give it any other treatment at all. Don't rub the surface hard, just keep the vacuum head close enough to the fabric to pick up dust.

- Embroidery and other delicate fabrics can be brushed very gently with a baby's hairbrush.

A-Z of Household Objects and Materials

This is a quick-reference chapter for items around the home that may not fit into another category or that need special treatment. If you look for an item here and don't find it, clean according to the material it is made of.

Acrylic plastics and fiberglass
Clean with warm detergent solution. Don't use abrasives. Don't use dry-cleaning solvents.

- Scratches can be concealed by polishing with a little metal polish.

Alabaster
Similar to marble. Often made into lamp bases and ornaments. Treat as for marble and be sure not to let liquid soak in because alabaster is porous.

Antiques
Care of antiques should be the same as for anything of similar materials except that you should treat the object with extreme respect, handle it ultra gently, and if you are in any doubt about how to treat it or what it is made of, or if it is damaged, take it to a professional.

Artificial flowers

Pour salt into a large paper bag. Put the flowers in, heads down. Shake vigorously. The dirt will be transferred to the salt.

• Many artificial flowers can be washed. Check when buying. Dunk them up and down in a bowl of warm water and mild detergent. Rinse in the same way.

Ash trays

Tip out all debris into the trash. Wash the ash tray (separately from the rest of the dishes) in warm, detergenty water. Then clean according to the material it is made of.

Baking tins/cookie sheets

• Wash in detergent and water and dry thoroughly.

• To remove burned-on food, boil the tin (if it is small enough to be put into a pot) for 3 to 5 minutes in water to which a little baking soda has been added. Alternatively soak the tins for several hours in detergent and water and wash them later.

• To remove rust marks, rub with a piece of cut raw potato dipped in flour or a mild abrasive.

Baskets

Vacuum thoroughly and frequently. Give them a good scrubbing with warm water about once a year, or turn the garden hose on them to prevent the cane from drying out and splitting. Dry thoroughly, preferably in the sun.

Baths

See page 85.

Books

Dust with the dusting brush of a vacuum cleaner or with a clean, soft, slightly damp paintbrush or make-up brush. Take each book off the shelf and dust outward from the binding. It is OK to flip the pages to dust them, but don't bang them together.

- Dry heat is not good for books as it damages the backings, pages, and bindings. A bowl of water will provide a little moisture in the air. Dampness on the other hand will cause mildew. If you have central heating, a humidifier in the room where the books are kept would help.

- Valuable antique books should be cleaned by a professional.

- Use saddle soap occasionally on leather bindings. Spread the soap quickly with your fingers or the palm of your hand or use a small piece of chamois, felt, or muslin. Be sparing and be careful not to touch the paper or cloth parts of the book. Massage it in gently until the soap has been absorbed. The leather will almost certainly be slightly darkened by this treatment but in centrally heated homes, particularly, it is a wise precaution to stop the leather from drying out.

- If molds begin to form on books move them from the damp air, or dry out the room. Fresh molds can be wiped off the bindings with a clean, soft cloth.

- Mildew on pages can be wiped off in the same way.

- Or slightly dampen the cloth with mineral spirits and spread the pages fanwise to dry.

- Or dust the mildewed pages with cornstarch, French chalk, fuller's earth, or talcum powder. Leave the powder in the closed book for several days, then brush it off.

- Books that have been left in the damp or damaged by flood should be treated bit by bit. Put sheets of tissue paper or paper towels between the pages. Put a weight on top and leave in warm, dry air or in a room with a fan heater directed toward them but not too close.

- Remove grease spots from a page by putting a paper towel on either side of the page and pressing gently with a warm iron.

Bottles
Fill with detergent and water and wash with a bottle brush.

• Babies' bottles should be cleaned with a sterilizing kit (electric or stovetop) according to the manufacturer's instructions.

Brooms and dustpan brushes

Wash in warm water and mild detergent with a little washing soda if they are very dirty. Then rinse a couple of times. If the broom is nylon or plastic, soak for five minutes in a bucket of water with 2 tablespoons of kitchen salt dissolved in it to stiffen the bristles.

Candlesticks

Don't use a knife to scrape off the wax. Pour warm water into the candle holder to soften the old wax so you can remove it more easily. To remove wax from the outer surface, push it off gently with a soft cloth wrapped around your finger.

• Don't sit weighted or hollow candlesticks in water.

Chandeliers

Dust frequently and clean them according to the material they are made of. Switch the electricity off at the circuit breaker. Unscrew every light bulb and clean each individually. While cleaning, check that the ceiling fixture and chain are in good condition.

• Wipe each pendant with cotton-gloved fingers dipped in a solution of vinegar and water or denatured alcohol and water.

• The lazy way to clean crystal chandeliers is to hold a glass of hot water and vinegar up to each pendant until it is immersed and then allow it to drip dry. Put a plastic tarp underneath to catch the drips.

China, porcelain, and pottery

Wash earthenware by machine (if dishwasher proof) or hand wash in clean, hot water and dishwashing liquid.

• Wash fine china by hand in a plastic bowl or tub to prevent chipping. Rinse and dry. Don't soak or rub hard or

use cleaning powders or scourers, which will damage the
glaze and the pattern.

- Cracks in fine porcelain can often be made less obvious
  by removing the dirt. Cover the crack with a cottonball or
  piece of cotton wool soaked in a solution of household
  ammonia or chlorine bleach. Leave it for several days,
  wetting the cotton from time to time with more solution.
  Scrub gently if necessary with a fine-bristle brush dipped
  in the solution.

- Don't pour cold water over hot china or hot water over
  cold china; it might crack or break due to the sudden
  change in temperature.

- Fine china, kept for display, should only be wiped occasionally first with a damp cloth and then a dry one.

- China with a raised pattern can be cleaned with an eyebrow or make-up brush kept for the purpose.

- Get rid of tea and coffee stains from china mugs, cups,
  and teapots by rubbing them with a soft wet cloth dipped
  in baking soda. There are some commercial products for
  removing these stains, but baking soda is cheaper and
  greener.

- Earthenware, stoneware, and salt-glaze ware are tougher
  than fine china, and often ovenproof and won't be harmed
  by very hot water or soaking. They can be washed satisfactorily in a dishwasher.

- Do not wash unglazed pottery. Just wipe with a damp
  cloth. Partially glazed bowls and dishes should be washed
  quickly by hand and not soaked.

- Check that china is dishwasher proof before putting it in
  your machine.

- Soaking old china in water may weaken the color and is
  especially damaging to any gold decoration.

- For general advice on dishwashing see Chapter 7.

Cloisonné
This is a form of enameling in which each part of the design
is outlined by bits of wire. Wash it as you would a piece of

fine china, with mild detergent and water. Rinse. Wipe dry
with a soft cloth. Don't use abrasives or harsh cleaners.

Clothespins

Wooden clothespins can be machine washed in a cotton bag
or pillow case. Nylon ones should be hand washed in a bowl
of hot water and dishwashing liquid.

Coffeemaker

Wash the inside every time you use the machine or traces of
oil from the last brew will give the new one a bitter taste.
Wipe the outside with a cloth wrung out in detergenty water.

- If there's an electric element don't get it wet.
- Don't dump coffee grounds down the drain. They will
  eventually clog it up, as will tea leaves.

Combs

Soak for a few minutes in 1 teaspoon of household ammonia
to 1 pint of warm water. Wash with a nailbrush. Rinse well.
Dry away from heat.

Coral

See Jewelry.

Corks

Sterilize in boiling water. Other cork objects, ice buckets for
instance, can be rubbed with fine sandpaper or an emery
board.

Cutlery

See pages 83, 137, and 156.

Decanters

See Glassware.

Diamonds

See Jewelry.

Electric blankets and heating pads

Wash or clean electric blankets according to the manufacturer's instructions. Don't use dry-cleaning solvents, which might damage the insulation wires.

- Don't use mothproofers on electric blankets because they may damage the wiring.

- Store in a plastic bag.

  Washable electric blankets. If you hand wash a blanket, shake it gently and soak it for 10–15 minutes in tepid water and mild detergent. Squeeze the suds gently through the fabric from time to time. Rinse two or three times in the same way. Do not wring or twist.

- If using a washing machine, fill the machine first with tepid water and agitate to dissolve the detergent. Then soak the blanket without tumbling for 15–20 minutes. Rinse in the same way. Gently pull the blanket into shape and hang to dry.

Electric heaters

Dust will make your heater less efficient and more expensive to run. Disconnect the electricity when dusting, cleaning, or polishing. If the heater has a fan, oil it every six months. Keep any reflectors brightly polished.

Emeralds

See Jewelry.

Enamel pots and pans

Enamel is a tough finish produced by fusing a special kind of glass onto a metal base. For cooking pans, baths, etc., the base is cast iron or steel. For jewelry it may be silver or gold (see Jewelry). Enamel can be chipped quite easily, and sudden changes of temperature may crack it, so cold pans should be heated slowly and hot pans should not be put down on a cold surface or filled with cold water.

- Wash enamel plates, bowls, mugs, etc., in warm water and

detergent. Do not use metal scrapers or scouring powders or anything abrasive. If food is stuck to the enamel, soak it in water for a few hours.

- You can safely use a nylon scourer on pans. If the food is burned on hard, fill the pan with water, add a teaspoon of baking soda and boil. Rinse and dry.

- Enamel does not like acid so don't let tomatoes, rhubarb, citrus fruits, or other acid foods sit in an enamel pan.

- Light stains can often be removed by rubbing the enamel with a damp cloth dipped in baking soda. Rinse and dry.

Eyeglasses
Wash occasionally with warm water and soap to remove accumulations of grease and oils from the skin and the atmosphere. Clean around the rims with a watercolor paintbrush. Give a final polish with an eyeglass-cleaning cloth or use tissues.

Flasks
Clean the inside with hot water and mild detergent or water and baking soda. Use a bottle brush if necessary. Rinse thoroughly. Leave the top off until the flask is next used to make sure it grows no mold. Don't immerse the flask in water, which might get between the interior and exterior or cause the metal casing to rust.

Glassware
- Add ¼ cup of white vinegar to dishwashing water to make glasses sparkle.

- Hot, white vinegar will remove paint spots from glass.

  Decanters, carafes, and narrow-necked vases. There are several methods of cleaning green mold, watermarks, and other stains that are difficult to remove from narrow-necked containers.

1. Shake tea leaves and vinegar in the vase together. Rinse and dry.

2. Fill with water plus 2 teaspoons household ammonia. Stand overnight. Wash and rinse.

3. Fill with a little sea sand or fine fish-aquarium gravel with a squirt of dishwashing liquid and warm water. Shake well. Leave for a few minutes, shake again. Continue until the sediment is loose.

Hairbrushes
Wash regularly in warm detergenty water. Brushes with nylon backs and nylon bristles can be boiled. Rinse well and dry away from direct heat.

Handbags
Keep handbags filled with crumpled newspaper when not in use to retain their shape.

Leather. Clean handles with saddle soap and then rub with leather conditioner. Polish briskly with a soft cloth.
• Use colored shoe polishes to restore color in worn areas.

Patent leather and suede. See Shoes and boots.

Plastic and vinyl. Wipe with a mild soap and water solution or use vinyl cleaner/conditioner.

Linings. Sprinkle with fuller's earth. Leave it to absorb the dirt and then vacuum or brush it out well. Or wipe the lining with a cloth wrung out in detergenty water and allow to dry naturally.

Hinges
All hinges should be checked and oiled from time to time. Remove dirt with a small clean paintbrush then smear with petroleum jelly, working it into the joints (use a cotton swab). This should stop squeaks and rusting. Remove surplus with tissues or paper towels.

Hot-water bottles
Rubber-ridged and fabric-covered hot water bottles may be soaked for two or three minutes in hot water and mild liquid detergent. Scrub with a soft nail brush or a sponge.

- The outside will dry more quickly if you fill them with hot water. Empty when dry.

- In summer store them away from light and heat, preferably hanging up. Always store them empty.

Ironing-board covers

Wash cotton covers like any other cotton material. Silicone covers should be dry-cleaned.

Irons

The bases of modern irons are either aluminium or chrome-plated and do not tarnish but may acquire residues of various elements that make them less smooth. It is essential to clean them immediately or ironing will be difficult and delicate fabrics may suffer.

- Disconnect the iron when you have finished ironing and before cleaning it.

- Let the iron cool in an upright position on its heel rest. Keep it like this when it is not in use during ironing sessions so you don't waste the steam.

- If the base has dried starch on it wipe it with a cloth wrung out in hot water and detergent.

- Remove melted nylon and other synthetic fibers by heating the iron then disconnecting it. While still hot wipe off the melted mess with a wooden (not plastic) spatula. Don't be tempted to use a sharp knife.

- From time to time rub the sole plate with beeswax and wipe off the surplus with a paper towel.

- If the opening of the sprinkler nozzle becomes blocked clear it with a fine sewing needle.

Ivory, bone, and horn items

Dust frequently with a soft cloth. Wipe with a mild detergent and water, then with a clean damp cloth; dry carefully. Never immerse in liquid.

- Knives with ivory handles should not be soaked in water.

Never put them in the dishwasher, just wash the blades; dry them as quickly as possible.

- All ivory will yellow with age. Daylight will delay this process but don't leave items out in hot sun, which also will dry and crack it.

Jade objects

Jade is a silicate of calcium or magnesium. It usually only needs to be dusted but if necessary wash in a lukewarm mild soapsud solution. Wash each piece separately in a plastic bowl.

Jewelry

Keep jewelry clean and store it carefully in separate boxes, not jumbled all together. Diamonds in particular can do a lot of damage to other pieces of jewelry, and gold and platinum scratch easily. If you don't have enough boxes or compartments, wrap each piece separately in acid free tissue paper (from jewelers), or cotton wool.

- As a general rule it is cheap and quite satisfactory to wash jewelry with warm water and a mild detergent, using a soft toothbrush to get into the intricate parts. A little household ammonia in the water helps to loosen the dirt. Don't use very hot water, which may expand the settings so that the stones fall out. Rinse in warm water and dry on a soft cloth with no loose threads that could catch on the setting.

- DO NOT use ammonia on pearls or coral.

- There are jewelry cleaning products on the market but they are, of course, more expensive than water and detergent. Follow the manufacturer's instructions. If in doubt, or for valuable and very old pieces seek professional advice first. The following hints concern specific kinds of jewelry:

  Acrylic jewelry. Sponge with lukewarm water and mild detergent. Wipe dry with a clean, damp cloth.
  - If scratched, use a little metal polish.

Amber. Wipe with a cloth wrung out in warm, soapy water and dry at once. Water makes amber cloudy, so don't leave it in the solution.
- Clean grease marks with a bread ball or by wiping over with safflower oil.

Bead necklaces. Restring about once a year.
- Clean stones and beads with dry baking soda on a soft brush.

Coral. Treat exactly as for pearls.

Costume jewelry. Wash in warm water (hot water may crack the stones). Don't leave in the water for very long or the cement may come loose. If it does, use an epoxy to glue it back in.

Diamonds. Take special care to keep diamonds clean so that the light will be reflected from each facet. Use an eyebrow brush or very soft toothbrush to loosen any dirt at the back of the setting.
- Diamonds may be boiled in a weak solution of soapsuds plus a few drops of ammonia. Place the object in a tea strainer or tie in a piece of muslin (like a bouquet garni) and dip it into the boiling liquid. Leave it there for just a moment. Remove and allow to cool. Dip it into ¼ cup of mineral spirits and lay it on paper towels to dry.

- Don't, of course, boil diamonds if there are other stones in the setting.

Emeralds. Washing may uncover hidden flaws and break the stones, so get them cleaned professionally.

Enamel. Dust very occasionally with a watercolor paintbrush. Don't use water that can get between the layers and damage the piece.

Glass. Wash in warm, detergenty water. Don't use hot or boiling water, which may crack the glass. Don't leave in water for too long in case it softens the setting. Use a soft brush to get into the crevices.
- You can polish glass bracelets, etc., with a silver cloth or a commercial stainless-steel cleaner.

- Rub scratches with a chamois leather and jeweler's rouge, pressing lightly.

Gold and platinum. Occasionally rub gently with a clean piece of chamois. Ordinary cloths may harbor bits of grit, which could damage the metal.

- Treat gold plate with the tenderest care because the actual gold is only a very thin layer that may wear off with excessive rubbing.

Ivory. Ivory absorbs liquid, swells up when wet, and may crack so don't wash it in water. Clean with cotton wool dipped in whiting and denatured alcohol.

- Give it a protective coating by rubbing it with a soft cloth dipped in safflower oil.

- You can slow up the yellowing process by keeping the ivory in the light. In the dark it will yellow much quicker.

- Bleach yellowed ivory by rubbing it with a cloth dipped in hydrogen peroxide and drying carefully with a soft cloth.

- Old ivory should be treated by a professional because you may ruin the patina.

Jet. This is a sort of glossy black lignite (brown coal) also known as black amber. It was enjoyed by the Victorians who wore it as a symbol of mourning when Prince Albert died.

- Soft breadcrumbs can be used to clean pieces of jet. If it is not decorated with materials that water damages, then it can be washed as for glass.

Opals. Opals are very brittle so handle them carefully, and don't expose them to extreme changes of temperature.

- Opals may be washed with warm water and mild detergent if not in a setting with materials that water damages.

Pearls. Most natural pearls are found in oysters, though a few are found in clams. The oyster is sometimes attacked by a minute parasitic worm and builds the pearl around it to relieve the irritation. The pearl is built up in thin layers of mostly calcium carbonate. Pearls therefore dissolve in acid. Cultured pearls are made by putting a tiny bit of mother-of-pearl inside an oyster, which duly covers it with pearl. Artificial pearls are made from hollow glass. The inside is covered with a special finish made from fish scales. If you want to test your pearls, real or cultured ones will feel rough if you draw them across your teeth. Artificial ones will feel smooth.

- Pearl necklaces should be restrung at least once a year or whenever they begin to get loose. Pearls are nearly always strung with a knot between each one, as are any valuable stones or beads, so that if the string breaks they all won't scatter over the ground.

- To clean pearls, rub them gently with a clean soft chamois leather, taking care to rub between the beads to remove the film of dirt picked up from you and the atmosphere every time you wear them.

- Individual pearls may be washed in warm water and mild detergent (NEVER ammonia) but pearl necklaces should not be washed because the water may damage the thread.

Precious and semi-precious stones. Rubies, amethysts, cairngorms, citrines, sapphires, turquoise, and garnets can all be washed using detergent and water.

Silver. Clean with a commercial silver polish. Do not leave any polish on the silver because that will cause it to tarnish again more quickly, and it will leave marks on your clothes.

- When cooking and washing up, remove silver rings because contact with egg, fruit juices, olives, perfumes, salad dressing, salt, vinegar, and so on all tarnish silver.

Wood. Wipe wooden beads, bangles, brooches, etc., with a barely damp cloth. Don't immerse in water because it may stain or warp the wood.

- Polish with a little wax polish or rub in a little olive oil. Use tiny amounts and be sure to wipe off any excess or it will stain your clothes.

Lacquered Items (ornamental trays, boxes, etc.)

Wipe over with a barely damp cloth. About once a year apply the tiniest amount of furniture wax on a clean soft cloth and polish gently with a second cloth.

• Lacquered furniture should only ever need dusting.

Lampshades

Dust regularly using a feather duster or the dusting brush of a vacuum cleaner.

Fiberglass shades. Wipe with a damp cloth.

Glass shades. Dust and wipe down with a cloth dipped in a solution of white vinegar and water.

Handpainted silk lampshades. Dry-clean only. Water will damage any pattern and leave marks.

Kitchen lampshades. Get dirtier and greasier than others. Use a strong detergent—carpet detergent, say, in a strong solution. Or you can use white vinegar.

Parchment shades. Real parchment is made out of the skins of goats or sheep and should be conditioned occasionally with neat's foot oil or castor oil to prevent it from drying out.
• Imitation parchment should be wiped with a damp cloth.

Plastic shades. Wipe with a cloth wrung out in soapy water, then wipe with a cloth wrung out in clear water and dry with a soft cloth.

Raffia and straw. Vacuum very frequently. They can be gently sponged with a just damp sponge from time to time.

Silk, nylon, and rayon lampshades. Wash them by hand, provided the shade is sewn and not glued to the frames and the trimmings are colorfast. Mix up a bowl of mild soap or detergent solution and dip the lampshade in and out. Rinse in the same way in tepid water. Stand the shade on a towel to dry, preferably in front of a fan heater because the quicker it dries, the less likely the frame is to rust.

- Silk, nylon, or rayon that is glued to the frame should be dry-cleaned before it gets too dirty.

Luggage, leather
Carefully dust or wipe the luggage with a soft cloth wrung out in soap suds (not detergent) or use saddle soap. Remove oily spots with a dry-cleaning solvent.

- Use neat's foot oil, lanolin, or castor oil to keep leather luggage supple. Use after cleaning and apply it while the leather is still slightly damp. Rub it in with the fingers or a pad of soft cloth then leave it to soak into the leather. Neat's foot oil is difficult to polish afterward, so if you want a polished finish use lanolin, castor oil, or a half and half combination of the two instead.

- Use white petroleum jelly on white or light luggage.

Marble objects and surfaces
Polished marble should only be dusted or wiped with a soft, damp cloth. Antique marble should be dealt with by a professional.

- Really filthy marble can be cleaned with a cloth wrung out in mild detergent and water, but don't use this method more than once or the marble may discolor. Dry with a chamois leather so as not to leave streaks.

- Always wipe up spilled food, drinks, cosmetics, etc., quickly since they are liable to stain the marble.

- Clean marks with lemon juice or vinegar, but don't leave it on for more than a minute or two. Repeat if necessary. Little and often is the rule. Rinse and dry immediately.

- Organic stains from tea, coffee, cosmetics, tobacco, leaves, colored paper, and ink can be bleached with hydrogen peroxide. Dab it on with cotton wool and watch carefully to see when it is having an effect so that you don't leave it on too long.

- Deep oily and greasy stains can be absorbed by making a paste of dry-cleaning solvent and whiting, leaving it on the stain for several hours, and then wiping it off. This is not guaranteed to remove stains but will help with some.

• Rust stains can be removed in the same way with a commercial rust remover added.

• Use commercial marble cleaners for light scratches.

Mirrors
See Chapter 10.

Mother-of-Pearl
This is the lining of sea shells. Clean it with soap and water. Don't use ammonia.

Musical Instruments
Keep musical instruments in their cases when they are not being played.

• Dust them with a clean, soft cloth and a very soft watercolor or eyebrow brush.

• Blow dust from the parts that are difficult to reach because of the strings, etc.

Music boxes
Keep cylinder music boxes out of direct sunlight and away from any form of heat or the glue that secures the mechanism may melt.

• Don't clean, oil, or touch the mechanism. If necessary take it to a professional repairer.

Paintbrushes
Use the thinner for whatever paint you are using: water-based paints need only water or detergent and water; lacquer needs a lacquer thinner or acetone; oil paints, varnishes and enamels need turpentine or mineral spirits; rubberized and synthetic-resin paints need detergent and water; shellac needs denatured alcohol, then soap and water. (Don't use mineral spirits to clean nylon brushes.) Pour a little of the solution onto the brush, work it in with gloved fingers and then paint as much

as possible onto old newspaper. Some brushes may have to be left in thinner overnight. Or use a commercial paintbrush cleaner that can deal with a number of different paints.

- Large brushes should be hung up by the handle. If you stand them on their heads, the hairs will be spread and distorted and if you stand them upside down the liquid flows back, weakening the mounting and making the hairs fall out. Drill a hole in the handle to hang the brush from. Or knock two nails into the wall about 1 inch apart to hold each brush.

- Smaller brushes can be stored flat if not hung up. Wrap the damp paintbrush in a kitchen towel to stop the bristles from splaying out.

- Don't allow brushes to sit in any solution or the bristles will bend and become loose.

- Add a fabric softener to the final rinse to help keep brushes soft and pliable.

Parchment
See Lampshades.

Pianos
Pianos are given a specially hard, shellac finish. Wipe with a soft cloth.

- Have the interior cleaned occasionally by a professional.

- Wipe the keys lengthways with a soft, slightly damp cloth, then dry with another soft cloth.

- Ivory keys will yellow with time. Sunshine helps to keep them white.

Pictures
Clean glass and frames with a cloth wrung out in water with a little white vinegar added. Don't get the water between the frame and the glass. Polish with paper towels or a chamois.

- Fly spots can be cleaned with cold tea.

- Apply wax polish to wooden picture frames if you wish or rub with a little olive oil.

Gilt frames. Clean with a cloth moistened with a little dry-cleaning fluid.

Oil paintings. Do not tamper with a painting you think may be valuable. Get it dealt with by a professional. Local art shops or dealers may be able to offer advice. The cleaning techniques and materials used will depend on the type of paint and canvas.

- Dust the painting by lightly brushing with a cotton rag, a soft brush or a feather duster. Don't use soap, water, breadcrumbs or any of the other erasers sometimes recommended. A very fine film of cream furniture polish may brighten the surface. Make sure the canvas is supported from the back while you are cleaning the front. Most experts disapprove of any further cleaning being done by amateurs.

Watercolor paintings. These are very difficult to clean so leave it to a professional. Erasers are too rough and crude but you can try a bread ball on a cheap watercolor.

Plastics

All plastics are easy to clean. Wipe them with a cloth wrung out in warm water and detergent.

Melamine. Used to make plates, cups, tumblers, jugs, cutlery handles, etc. It is strong, good-looking, tasteless, non-toxic, and doesn't smell. Boiling water will not damage it and it can be put in the dishwasher. However it does stain rather easily.

- Remove stubborn stains with a little toothpaste rubbed on with your finger or an old toothbrush. Don't use scouring powders or pads because melamine scratches easily.

- Baking soda will often remove light stains.

Nylon plastic. This is a very tough plastic. It is opaque or nearly white or tinted. It is not affected by freezing, is lightweight and rigid, but slightly resilient. It is used for plastic cups, brushes, and bristles.

- Nylon utensils and dishes can be put in the dishwasher, and nylon brushes can be boiled. (If you are not sure if they are nylon, don't boil them or put them in the dishwasher because acrylic and ordinary plastic won't stand up to such treatment.)

- Nylon utensils used for coffee or tea should be washed quickly before they become permanently stained. Don't use abrasives. Don't use them for cooking.

Playing cards

Paper cards should be wiped carefully with a cotton ball moistened with mineral spirits and dried with clean tissues or paper towels.

- Plastic cards only need to be wiped with a damp cloth.

Records and compact discs (CDs)

Clean records with a soft cloth moistened with a solution of lukewarm water and mild detergent. Then wipe with a cloth squeezed out in clear water. Wipe dry with a lint-free cotton or linen cloth.

- Clean CDs underneath with a cloth squeezed out in warm, detergenty water. Wipe dry with a lint-free cloth.

Shoe brushes

Soak in a solution of warm water and detergent containing a little household ammonia. Wash. Rinse well and dry with the head down.

- If the brush is caked with hardened shoe polish, soak it in a saucer of mineral spirits, rub it on newspaper or old rags, and then wash it again.

Shoes and boots

Leather. Remove surface dirt with a soft brush. If the shoes are muddy wait for the mud to dry and then remove it with a stiff brush. Any remaining mud can be removed with a soft, damp cloth.

- Apply polish with a soft brush or shoe cream with a soft cloth.

- Buff up with a medium brush.

- Finish off by using a buffer (a small pad covered in velvet) for a high shine.

Patent leather. Clean with a soft cloth wrung out in detergenty water. Buff up with a soft dry cloth. Wax will crack the leather but you can wipe a little milk over the surface and then buff up for extra shine.

Suede. Brush with a special bristle, rubber or wire suede brush, working in a circular motion. Rub gently or you will damage the surface.

Slate

Wash slate worktops with mild detergent and water then apply a little lemon oil to make it lustrous. Wipe with a clean cloth after applying the oil to remove all excess.

- Instead of oil you can apply milk to give a lustre. Rub it down well afterward with a clean cloth.

- Slate on worktops can be sealed with a special sealant, which will keep the surface smooth, dark, and dust free.

Soap dishes

Soak for a few minutes in a solution of 1 tablespoon washing soda dissolved in half a gallon of very hot water. Scrub with a dishwashing brush or a nail brush. Rinse and dry.

Sponges and loofahs

Sea sponges. Wash in warm soapy water or detergent and water. If they have become slimy with soap, boil them in water and detergent. Allow to cool, squeeze out well, and rinse. Don't bleach.
- Or soak overnight in salt water or baking soda and water then wash in the dishwasher.

Plastic sponges. These can be cleaned with a mild household ammonia solution of 1 tablespoon per quart of water.

This sometimes improves the color and certainly disinfects them. Don't use strong bleaches or strong detergents. A weak solution of dishwashing liquid and a weak solution of hydrogen peroxide should be OK.

- Synthetic or rubber sponge mops should be soaked before using because they are brittle when dry. Rinse well after use and hang up to dry naturally, away from direct heat or sunlight.

Sun lamps

Keep the reflectors brightly polished to reflect as much heat as possible. Use a polish-impregnated wadding.

Taps

Keep chrome taps clean with a few drops of liquid paraffin applied on a damp cloth. Paraffin dries quickly leaving no drips and the smell disappears almost at once. Metal polish is not necessary.

- Or use vinegar or lemon juice.

Teapots

Aluminum. Fill with water and 2 tablespoons borax; boil and then wash as usual.

China. Clean inside with a cloth moistened with water and dipped in baking soda. Rinse in very hot water.

Chrome. Clean inside with a cloth moistened with white vinegar and dipped in salt. Rinse in very hot water.

Silver. Clean the inside with hot water and borax. Use ½ teaspoon borax to 1 pint water. Leave for an hour then clean with a dishwashing brush. Use a bottle brush for the spout. Rinse thoroughly. Clean the outside as you would for silver (see page 156).

Telephones

Dust telephones frequently. Wipe over from time to time with a damp cloth wrung out in detergent and water. Dry with a soft, clean cloth.

Televisions

Unplug before attempting to clean. Clean the screen with a cloth wrung out in mild detergent and water. The cloth should be barely damp. Dry with a clean, lint-free cloth.

- Don't use solvents, chemical cleaners, or polishes, which can damage the screen. Make sure dust rags have no grit in them, which could cause scratches.

Tortoiseshell

Clean with jeweler's rouge; rub on gently with a soft cloth. Leave for a few minutes then polish with a clean dust rag.

- Imitation tortoiseshell may be washed in warm, soapy water then rinsed and dried.

Trash cans and garbage cans

Line all cans with plastic or paper bags. Remove the bags and seal them up before they become too full. This will keep the can much cleaner and you will have to wash it less often.

- The greener way is to wrap garbage in old newspaper and put it in the unlined can.

- Wash the can with hot water and detergent, using a little disinfectant if it is needed. Dry and air well.

- Grind half a lemon in a food processor and put it in the trash to counteract unpleasant smells.

Typewriters

Unplug electric typewriters before cleaning. Remove the platen and wipe it and the little rubber rollers that feed in the paper with dry cleaning solvent on a clean cloth. Brush out the dust and gunk from the platen holder.

- Clean the type with commercial cleaning fluid or mineral spirits. Slip a piece of folded paper under the type bars and scrub the type with a stiff typewriter brush or an old toothbrush. You can get spray-on cleaners or doughy cleaners for this job too. For golf-ball and daisy-wheel typewriters follow the manufacturer's instructions.

• Move the carriage to the extreme left and put one drop of oil on the tracks. Do not oil the type bars.

Vases
Wash the insides with warm water and detergent, and if necessary use straight white vinegar to clean off the green gunk and hard water marks. Leave the vinegar in the vase for 5 or 10 minutes, then clean with a bottle brush, rinse, and dry. For narrow-necked vases see Glassware.

VCRs
Clean as for a television set. Keep the cover on to prevent dust from getting into the mechanism.

Venetian blinds
Wear a pair of cotton gloves and run the slats between your fingers and thumb. If the slats need more than just a dust, dip them in detergent solution first.

Window shades
Rub with a terry-cloth rag dipped in flour.

Wooden bowls, boxes, etc.
Don't wash in water, which will be absorbed and crack the wood. Wipe over with a barely damp cloth. Clean dust from carvings with a soft brush.

• Rub with a tiny quantity of olive oil and lemon juice if necessary. See also Jewelry.

A-Z of Cleaning Metals

Many metals tarnish easily, or can be easily scratched and become worn. Certain metals, such as copper (in roofs), bronze, and pewter, may be admired for the patination they acquire with age, but most metals will benefit from regular care and attention and will last longer when protected from rust and corrosion.

Aluminum
Aluminum is made from naturally occurring alumina.

- Wash aluminum pans in mild detergent and water. Rinse in hot water and drain or dry with a soft tea towel. Burned-on food should be left to soak then scraped off with a wooden spoon or spatula and cleaned with a soap-filled steel-wool pad. Aluminum cooking items can be washed in a dishwasher.

- Dull aluminum pans can be brightened by boiling up water in the pan with a tablespoon of white vinegar.

- Or add a teaspoon of cream of tartar to 1 pint of water, bring to the boil and simmer for a couple of minutes.

- Don't keep food in an aluminum pan after cooking. Chemicals in the food may cause the metal to corrode and spoil the pan's looks as well as contaminating the food.

- Aluminum roasting pans need a lot of scouring to get rid of burned-on grease.

Brass

An alloy of copper and zinc.

- If very dirty wash first with detergent and water.

- Traditionally brass was cleaned with oxalic acid and salt but oxalic acid is highly poisonous and so is not to be recommended. The right way is to use a commercial brass polish, and follow the manufacturer's instructions.

- The lazy way is to buy lacquered brass, which just needs an occasional wash in warm water and detergent. Unfortunately the lacquer often becomes damaged and the metal will then corrode under the remaining lacquer. All the lacquer will have to be removed in order to clean the brass before the item is re-lacquered. This is difficult to do and best done by a professional.

- The green way is to apply a paste of white vinegar and salt, or a piece of lemon. Leave on for five minutes or so, then remove and wash carefully. Dry then polish with an essential oil (from chemists or herbal shops) applied on a soft cloth.

- Very dirty objects such as fire tongs may have to be rubbed with steel wool or very fine emery cloth. Rub the metal up and down, not around in a circle. It will take some time. Rinse thoroughly in hot water and detergent and dry.

- Brass preserving pans (for making jams and preserves) should be cleaned inside with a paste of vinegar and kitchen salt. Wash and rinse thoroughly after cooking anything in them and dry well. Metal polish should never be used on the inside of a brass pan, which is intended for cooking, but you can use it for the outside.

- Old brass pans that have not been used recently should be cleaned professionally if you intend to use them for cooking.

Bronze

An alloy of copper and tin.

- Bronze should never be washed or it might corrode irreparably. Don't touch the surface at all except to dust it lightly and even then very infrequently.
- Bronze corrodes easily, forming a light green or sometimes even red, black, or blue patina. This patination in antique bronzes is considered to be desirable. Antique bronzes require professional treatment.
- Nowadays solid bronze is often lacquered in the factory. Bronze with this sort of finish will only need dusting and, occasionally, a wipe with a damp cloth. If the lacquer cracks or peels it will have to be removed and the object re-lacquered.

Cast Iron

Wash in warm, soapy water, dry immediately, then coat with vegetable oil and keep in a dry place to prevent rust.

- Don't use harsh abrasives or metal scrapers.
- Don't run cold water into a hot pan.
- Don't store with the lid tightly on.

Chromium

A soft, silvery metal that does not tarnish in air and can be highly polished.

- Wipe with a soft, damp cloth and polish with a dry one.
- Very dirty chrome can be washed with warm water and detergent. Dry thoroughly afterward.
- The right way to clean chrome is to use a chrome cleaner from a car and bike accessory shop or hardware store.
- You can use a little paraffin applied on a damp cloth to clean fly-blown or greasy chrome.
- The green way is to use baking soda on a damp cloth.

Copper
A lustrous red-brown metal.

- In air, copper forms a greenish surface film that can cause nausea and vomiting if eaten. So copper pans must be kept scrupulously clean and should never have food left standing in them. Most modern copper pans are lined with chromium or tin. Some even have a non-stick surface.

- Do not cook food containing vinegar, lemon juice, rhubarb, or other acids in an unlined copper pan as they will react with the metal and taint the food.

- Wash copper utensils and ornaments with water and detergent, rinse, and dry well.

- Use a nylon scourer or nylon brush to clean burned-on food.

- Polish the exterior the right way with commercial copper cleaner.

- The lazy way is to reduce the need to polish by having the copper lacquered.

- Polish the green way using vinegar or lemon juice and salt; or equal parts of salt, vinegar, and flour; or buttermilk. Rinse at once and dry well.

Gold
See Jewelry, page 138.

Pewter
Pewter is an alloy of tin and various other metals, which may include lead, antimony, copper, bismuth, and zinc.

- Ordinary pewter can be polished with a suitable metal polish about two or three times a year.

- If kept in a humid atmosphere, pewter will quickly develop what's called a "hume" with a gray film and tarnishing. Tarnish can be removed by immersing the item in solvent chemicals but only a specialist should do this.

Platinum
See Jewelry, page 138.

Silver
A precious metal that is soft, white, lustrous, and easily worked. Sterling silver contains at least 925 parts of silver to 75 parts of copper.

Silver needs constant care. It is best when used every day as constant use gives it a rich and mellow lustre. Nevertheless it will tarnish eventually. A damp, polluted or salty atmosphere will speed up the tarnishing. You can buy various bags, wraps, and rolls of tarnish-inhibiting cloth and acid-free tissue paper to store silver in. These are available from jewelers. Don't store silver in plastic bags or plastic wrap, and don't use rubber bands for securing the wrapping as rubber can corrode silver through several layers of cloth and the damage will be permanent.

- Wash silver as soon as you can after it has been used, in hot water and dishwashing liquid. Rinse in hot water and dry at once.

- Wear cotton gloves when cleaning silver and treat the pieces gently. Old silver has often been worn leaf thin because it was cleaned with homemade, slightly abrasive products using whiting. Modern treatments should only remove the tarnish.

- Don't use silver cleaner on metals other than silver, gold, or platinum.

- The right way to clean tarnished silver is to rub it with a commercial silver polish using a soft cloth. There are paste, liquid, or powder polishes, tarnish-retardant polishes, dips, and impregnated cloths and gloves.

- When polishing rub each piece briskly but not too hard, using even, firm, straight strokes.

- One way of cleaning silver-plated cutlery that is in daily use and for cleaning etched and embossed pieces is to use a dip product. If you can't get the object into the dip jar, dab it with a cotton ball saturated in the solution. Don't leave items in the dip longer than necessary.

• Antique silver should be washed in warm water with a little mild detergent. Dry thoroughly with muslin, paper towels or old, soft linen tea-towels. Do not use new linen cloths because the starch in them is too abrasive. When thoroughly dry, clean with a commercial long-term silver cloth.

• Heavily tarnished antique silver should be treated with a silver dip applied with cotton swabs, following the manufacturer's instructions. Dry with a soft muslin or linen cloth and polish with a long-term silver cloth. When dealing with a large object clean a small area at a time, rinsing off the silver dip before going on to clean the next area. Don't use the same solution indefinitely because it becomes overcharged with silver, which eventually gets deposited back on the surface as matt silver.

• Clean small objects with a brush specially made for cleaning silver. The bristles of toothbrushes or other household brushes are too rough and will scratch the surface.

• The lazy way of cleaning silver is to concoct your own electrolytic silver cleaner, which is quick, simple, non-smelly, time saving, and harmless but disapproved of by jewelers because it leaves the silver somewhat white and lusterless. Don't use it on antique silver or silverware with handles that may be fastened with cement.

1. Fill a bowl with hot water.

2. Dissolve a handful of washing soda or baking soda in the water.

3. Add a handful of silver bottle tops or aluminum foil (or use an aluminum pan instead of a bowl).

4. Put in the silver making sure it is completely covered. Watch this brew seethe as the electro-chemical reaction removes the tarnish from the silver and deposits it on the aluminum. It should only take two or three minutes.

Stainless steel

Stainless steel is an iron alloy containing chromium. It is rust proof, but salt and acids can cause pit marks if left in contact with it for too long.

- Wash stainless steel in hot water and detergent, rinse and dry.
- Corroded spots on cooking pans can be cleaned off with fine steel wool and a fine scouring powder. Polish with a soft cloth. Special stainless steel cleaners are available.
- Clean dulled stainless steel utensils with a stainless steel polish. Don't use steel wool on silverware.

  Steel wool pads. Those without soap often get rusty. To prevent them from rusting, keep them in a cup of water with 3 tablespoons of baking soda.

Tempered steel

Wash immediately after use and dry meticulously to prevent rusting. Scour with wire wool and scouring powder from time to time and keep knives well sharpened.

Wrought Iron

Polish with liquid wax to prevent rust or treat with a rust inhibitor and then paint it with a paint specially made for iron.

- Remove rust spots with steel wool dipped in paraffin.

14

A-Z of Household Pests

One way to discourage pests is not to provide anything for them to eat or nest in. So wipe up crumbs after each meal, keep all food covered, do the dishes regularly, and don't leave uneaten cat or dog food on the floor. Fill cracks or holes in floors and walls. Don't allow stagnant water to collect near the house, disinfect your garbage bin, tie up all bags with garbage in them before putting them out of doors, and keep the bin covered. Clean drains weekly with washing soda crystals and boiling water.

This chapter suggests methods for dealing with specific unwanted pests in or near the house. If you are really plagued by pests such as rats or mice, or have a wasps' or bees' nest in the roof, you can call in a professional exterminator.

Always follow the manufacturer's instructions when using insecticides and store out of reach of children. Don't use near food (e.g., cover fruit bowls before spraying). If you get any on your skin, wash it off at once. On no account let any get near your mouth.

Ants
Follow their path back to the nest and destroy it with a suitable insecticide, following instructions, or by pouring boiling water over it.

- Or deter them by blocking up the entrance hole with a piece of cotton wool soaked in paraffin. Then spray floor, beneath baseboards, sinks, and windowsills with insecticide. Take care pets and children can't get at it.

- Don't leave jams, sugars, and fats where ants can find them.

Bedbugs

These lice-like insects hide during the day in cracks in walls and ceilings and appear at night to prey on you. They may be found in mattress seams, crevices in headboards and bed frames, behind window and door frames, baseboards, picture moldings, furniture, loose wallpaper, and cracks in plaster.

- Use an insecticide but make sure it is suitable—too high a concentration of some insecticides is dangerous to humans. Spray it into all possible hiding places (bedsprings, frames, webbing, and slats of beds) so they are thoroughly wet. Spray but don't soak the mattress, paying particular attention to seams and tufts. Spray baseboards and cracks in walls and floor boards.

- At any sign of another bedbug, spray the whole lot again with equal thoroughness. Better still, throw out or burn the mattress and get a new one.

- If in despair call an exterminator.

Fleas

Fleas will multiply readily in clean or squalid conditions if the house is warm enough. All pets who go outdoors will pick up fleas at some time. Infection with fleas may lead to dermatitis or tapeworm, and fleas may produce a violent allergic reaction in some dogs and cats.

- If an animal scratches a lot, check it for fleas. Part the hair and look for the fleas scurrying away or for their dandruff-like droppings.

- Buy flea powders from a vet rather than a pet shop and always follow the manufacturer's instructions.

- Do not use flea powders intended for use on one sort of animal on another. Cats in particular can absorb a number of toxic substances through their skin, and both cats and dogs may be made ill by preparations wrongly applied. Don't let the powder come into contact with the animal's eyes or mouth.

• While treating your pet make sure you clean the house thoroughly at the same time; flea eggs can produce larvae in two to twelve days in warm conditions but may remain dormant for two months or much longer in cool temperatures. Vacuum thoroughly especially in crevices, upholstery, baseboards, cushions, and anything soft and warm. Burn the contents of the vacuum bag or seal it up in a plastic bag.

• Wash, burn, or throw away the animal's bedding and use disposable bedding until the fleas have gone. Replace every few days.

Flies

Flies can spread at least 30 different diseases to animals and people. They breed in garbage and rotting meat, especially in hot weather.

• Keep all food and garbage tightly covered. Keep trash cans clean. Make sure animal feces are picked up or covered up.

• There are various suitable insecticides. All must be used strictly according to the manufacturer's instructions.

• Fly papers are effective and don't pollute the environment.

Mice

Mice are unhygienic and smelly. They eat breads, cereals, sugar, and cheese, chew wires, and leave their droppings everywhere.

• Block any holes they may come in by (often under the sink and inside cupboards where the pipes run).

• Keep all food in sealed jars and tins.

• Keep all garbage tightly covered.

- Keep a cat. Often just the catty smell will keep mice at bay.

- Set traps. Peanut butter, cheese, bacon, and cake make good bait. Put the traps at right angles to the walls where you know mice visit and where children and pets can't get at them.

- Or use an anticoagulant poison specifically formulated for mice. Follow the instructions carefully. You may have to persevere for several weeks. Take care to put the poisons where they cannot be reached by the innocent.

- Other poisons are highly dangerous and should only be used by professionals.

Moths

Natural fibers are susceptible to moth larvae, which can ruin clothes and curtains etc., by eating them. Man-made fibers are moth proof but, if blended with natural fibers, the material is still susceptible to damage. Clothes in daily use are not usually attacked but fabric items that are stored are at risk, especially if they are not washed or cleaned before being put away.

- Clear out all cupboards and chests, vacuuming up dust, which moths breed in.

- Store clothes in plastic garment bags so moths can't get at them.

- Use spray-on moth repellents. Or use moth repellent sachets or moth balls.

- The green way to keep moths at bay is to use camphor or turpentine. Alternatively place a mixture of cloves, cinnamon, black pepper, and orris root in small muslin bags and store these among the clothes. Or use dried orange peel or a few drops of lavender oil.

Rats

Rats will appear wherever there is food or somewhere to make a nest. Old rags left to rot in a shed will encourage them, so will open garbage cans or compost heaps containing too much food waste.

- Deal with the occasional rat by using poisoned bait. Some rats are developing an immunity to poisons and it may be sensible to use two different kinds: anticoagulants and multiple-dose poisons. Follow the directions very carefully and don't let children or pets get anywhere near the poisons. Remove dead rats at once by placing them in a plastic bag, sealing it up and putting it in the garbage.
- If you are worried about a rat infestation, don't hesitate to hire a professional.

Silverfish
These are silvery insects about half an inch long, found on the floor in damp, cool places. They feed on sugar and starch and can damage books and rayon.

- Use a household insecticide, in spray or powder form, around doors, windows, skirtings, cupboards, and pipes.

Spider
Spiders are your friends. They will eat flies and other unfriendly insects and are usually harmless.

Water bugs
Big black beetles that lurk under refrigerators and other dark corners and appear at night to eat food, starch, fabrics, and paper.

- Sprinkle infested areas with pyrethrum powder.
- If the infestation is bad, spray with a suitable insecticide and then sprinkle the powder, carefully blowing or fanning it into cracks and openings.

15

A-Z of Household Products

A great many chemicals are used in household cleaning products, and there are some that can be bought in pure form and used in a more diluted form, which work just as well. There are also a few natural products that can do most of the household cleaning, which are safer, more environmentally sound, and cheaper.

This guide is intended to be a quick reference to household cleaning substances as well as to some chemicals found in household cleaners, what they are made of, what they do, and when it is appropriate to use them.

It is still not always easy to get such information from labels on products. If in doubt write to the manufacturer for a list of contents.

Abrasives
Anything rough or gritty used to rub out stains or raise the nap of a fabric, such as whiting, pumice, scourers, and sandpaper, etc.

Absorbents
Anything that will soak up liquids (salt, fuller's earth, French chalk, talcum powder, tissues, etc).

Acetic acid (vinegar)
A colorless liquid used to brighten colored fabrics by rinsing

away alkaline residues caused by hard water, which makes colored fabrics dull. Buy it from the pharmacy or a photo store, and dilute it in the proportions of 1 tablespoon to 1 gallon of water. Vinegar is a diluted, impure form of acetic acid but does many cleaning jobs very well.

Acetone

A solvent for animal and vegetable oils and for nail polish. Also a useful paint remover. Do not use on acetate fabrics as it will dissolve them. Available from the drugstore. Highly flammable.

Acids and alkalis

Acidity/alkalinity is measured by a number from 0 to 14 called pH. Pure water is pH7 or neutral. Acidity is below 7, alkalinity above 7.

Acids. Dissolve in water producing a sour solution (though many acids are far too poisonous to taste) and turn litmus paper red. The acids used in cleaning (acetic acid, citric acid) are usually mild. Water can be alkaline or acid. Too much alkali in the wash water can change the colors in fabrics. Acids can counteract this color change.

Alkalis (ammonia, caustic soda [lye], TSP, and other soda compounds). Soluble in water. Alkaline water tastes bitter, feels slippery and turns litmus paper blue. Alkalis neutralize acids, will rot animal and vegetable substances (wool and silk or rayon for instance), and will change colors in many dyes.

Mild alkali soaps have a pH of 8–10. Soapless detergents can have a pH of almost 7 (neutral). Strong alkali laundry detergents may have a Ph of 10–11 and are best used for cotton and linen. Wool, silk, rayon, and colored fabrics need a pH of between 7 and 8.

Air fresheners and air purifiers

Some conceal odors with their own. Others actually destroy smells by reacting with them chemically. There are aerosol air fresheners, some that refresh from a wick, some that hang inside the toilet tank, and some that release their odor gradually when opened. A clean home should not need air fresheners or purifiers, but they may be useful to counteract the smell if someone's been sick or the cat has been caught short indoors. If you want to be green don't use the aerosols.

• Air purifiers contain an antiseptic ingredient such as triethylene glycol.

Alcohol (Isopropyl, denatured, or grain)
A large class of organic chemicals. Alcohol is useful in cleaning because it dissolves grease and evaporates rapidly. Useful for cleaning glass.

Alkalis
See Acids and alkalis.

Ammonia
A colorless gas with a pungent, penetrating odor. Dissolves readily in water to form ammonium hydroxide, which is an alkali and grease solvent. Buy household ammonia, which is ammonia solution specially prepared for domestic use.

• Do not use ammonia on silk, wool, aluminum, or sisal.

• Wear gloves while using ammonia. Don't sniff the liquid, and handle with caution. If you get any on the skin or near the eyes, wash off with plenty of cold water. Then use a diluted acid (½ level teaspoon boric acid to 1 pint water) for the eyes and a stronger solution (1 tablespoon to 1 pint water) for the skin.

• Many metal polishes contain ammonium hydroxide, which removes any metal oxides, especially of copper.

Amyl acetate (banana oil)
A solvent for celluloid and cellulose paint and nail polish. Available from the drugstore. It smells of peardrops. Should be safe on acetate fabrics unless what is spilled on them contained acetone and the fabric is already damaged. Inflamma-

ble and toxic; don't breathe fumes and keep windows open when using.

Baking soda
See Sodium bicarbonate.

Bathroom and kitchen cleaners
Various different types including foam cleaners and liquid cleaners. Some may be slightly abrasive. Kitchen cleaners will contain more alkali, bathroom cleaners more acid.

Powder cleaners, which are based on sodium acid sulphate, should never be used on any surface other than the toilet bowl as they are corrosive.

* Bleach is often used as a cheap cleaner and disinfectant for toilet bowls.
* Caustic soda is also used in some bathroom cleaners.
* Don't use two different lavatory cleaners together because the result may be toxic or explosive or both.
* For everyday cleaning, a vinegar and water solution can be quite satisfactory for the bathroom (see page 86).

Beeswax
Obtained from honeycombs. Sold in blocks in drugstores or hardware stores. Used in some furniture polishes.

* Make your own furniture polish with 1 ounce beeswax to ¼ pint turpentine. Scrape the beeswax into the turpentine and leave to dissolve for several days. Shake well before using.

Blue or washing blue
This is a water-soluble blue dye. A tiny bit in the wash will make yellowish fabrics look white. Many powdered laundry detergents contain small amounts of blue anyway. But there are cheap powder blues and liquid blues available from some supermarkets should you want to use them.

Borax

A white crystalline alkali mineral salt slightly soluble in water. Used as a water softener in laundry, bath, and shampoo products and as an antiseptic. It loosens dirt and grease and retards the growth of many molds and bacteria.

Builders

Substances added to laundry detergents to increase cleaning efficiency. They include sodium carbonate, borax, sodium silicate, and sodium phosphates. "Built" soaps should not be used for washing the face or hands or washing delicate fabrics.

Carbolic acid (phenol)

A weak acid and a powerful disinfectant. Used in general disinfectants for cleaning floors, drains, and toilets and in timber preservatives. Cresols are similar. The efficiency of a disinfectant is measured against phenol, which is used as a standard comparison.

Carbon tetrachloride

This has no place nowadays in the household. It is extremely poisonous.

Castor oil

Comes from the bean of the castor oil plant. Good leather conditioner, especially for polished leather.

Caustic soda (lye, or sodium hydrate, or sodium hydroxide)

A strong alkali used for cleaning ovens and bad stains on baths and sinks. Can be bought as a jelly or as a stick cleaner or a liquid. Used in many lavatory cleaners and for unblocking drains.

- Do not use it to clear kitchen sink outlets, because it could combine with grease to form a hard soap, which will block the drain completely. Use washing soda and boiling water instead.

- Caustic soda will burn through cloth, enamel, bristle brushes, rubber gloves, and damage aluminum. When using caustic soda, follow the manufacturer's instructions carefully. Don't get it on the skin or near the eyes. If you do, wash with lots of cold water.

Chlorine bleach

Sodium hypochlorite is a chlorine compound used in household bleaches. It has a characteristic and suffocating smell. Useful for bleaching white cottons, linens, and synthetics but do not use on silk, wool, mohair, leather, elasticated drip-dry, or other resin-treated fabrics. Always test a sample of the fabric first. Even cotton and linen will weaken if left in the solution too long. Follow manufacturer's instructions.

- Chlorine bleach will remove stains from baths, sinks, enamelware, tiles, and woodwork. Use about 2 tablespoons to 1 pint water. If necessary soak cotton wool or tissues in the solution and leave it on the stain for 5 minutes or so.

- If you use bleach as a bathroom cleaner do not use other cleaners at the same time. Chlorine and ammonia and other preparations used in bathroom cleaners produce a chemical reaction and a poisonous gas that can be very dangerous.

- Chlorine bleach can lose its effectiveness if stored for too long.

Citric acid (lemon juice)

A mild acid that can be used to counteract alkali stains, remove hard water scale, clean brass, etc.

Denatured alcohol

Ethyl alcohol with an additive such as methanol. Dissolves some paint, essential oils, castor oil, shellac and certain dyes, ballpoint pen ink, iodine, grass stains, and some medicines. Useful for cleaning mirrors and glass objects. Highly flammable, poisonous.

Descaling products

Used for removing fur or scale caused by minerals in hard water. Coffeemakers, kettles, hot water tanks, steam irons, and water pipes are all likely to get furred up if you live in a hard-water area. Commercial descalers are available from hardware stores. Follow the manufacturer's instructions carefully. Some descalers can be used on their own, others have to be used with household ammonia.

- It's not necessary to buy special products though. A tablespoon of borax to a kettleful of water will descale the kettle and so will vinegar (see page 82).

Detergents

Traditionally the word detergent describes any substance that cleans surfaces or removes dirt. Nowadays soap-based detergents are called soap and synthetic detergents are called detergents. Most synthetic detergents are based on petroleum by-products. Additives or builders of various kinds are added to many detergents to make them clean better and to prevent dirt being redeposited on the fibers. Perfumes and bleaches are also included. An important feature of detergents is their degree of alkalinity (see Acids and alkalis). Most household detergents are neutral as this does little damage to surfaces or skin, but the higher the pH value of a detergent, the better it is at removing dirt.

- Synthetic detergents dissolve easily in hot or cold water and are effective in hard water without the use of water softeners. They do not create scum and don't leave a film on washed surfaces or in bowls or buckets.

- Detergents vary in strength and blueness, etc. Too much detergent will eventually make clothes grayish and colored clothes dull because of the added blue. Other additives may include: a cellulose dirt-suspending agent, builders (mainly phosphates), suds stabilizers, metal protector to prevent corrosion of aluminum, oxygen bleach, enzymes, fluorescent whitening agents (which only work properly on thoroughly clean fibers), coloring, and perfume. Heavy duty detergents have the most additives.

- Greener detergents are those that have the fewest, if any, phosphates, bleaching agents, enzymes, and perfumes.

Disinfectants

Used to kill or prevent germs and bacteria on surfaces (as opposed to antiseptics, which are used in or on the body).

The first disinfectants used in surgery were carbolic acid solutions. Then cresols and phenols were found to be more effective, and in 1930 chloroxylenol was evolved. The main types of disinfectants used in homes and in cleaning products today are: chlorine bleaches, hydrogen peroxide, phenol, cresol, chloroxylenol, quaternary ammonium compounds, and triethylene glycol.

Enzymes

See Detergents.

Fabric softeners

Sometimes called fabric conditioners. Used in laundry rinse water to make textiles soft and fluffy and less likely to crease and to help reduce static electricity especially in synthetic fibers. They must be used with each wash.

- Try to find non-perfumed ones.

Fluorocarbons

Wide range of synthetic chemicals used in commercial drycleaning solvents. They are in the process of being withdrawn because their manufacture damages the ozone layer but will probably be with us for another ten years.

French chalk (tailor's chalk, clay chalk, wax chalk, soapstone, or steatite)

A compact kind of talc with a soapy feel. Powdered French chalk can be used as an absorbent for soaking up fresh grease stains from fabrics. It is quite harmless to all fabrics and will not leave a mark. Available through a tailor, a sewing shop, or cleaning supply wholesalers.

Fuller's earth
Clay mineral used as an absorbent, to remove grease from unwashable fabrics. Available at hardware stores.

Graphite
Used for blacking grates, etc. It is a natural crystalline form of carbon and nothing to do with lead. Modern versions are available in tubes.

Hydrogen peroxide
A disinfectant and a bleach available from drugstores in a diluted solution (usually in 20 parts its own volume of water) which should be further diluted for use at home. Will damage fabric and skin if left in contact too long or used in too strong a solution.

Isopropyl (rubbing) alcohol
A solvent sometimes used instead of denatured alcohol for dissolving lacquer, varnish, shellac, and removing ballpoint pen marks.

Lanolin
A sticky yellow wax obtained from sheep fleece. It is mainly a mixture of fatty acids, alcohols, and cholesterol. Can be used as a conditioner for leather.

Linseed oil
An oil from common flax seeds with practically no taste or smell. Used for making oil paints, varnishes, and furniture polishes and for oiling natural wood. Boiled linseed oil is darker and has a strong, characteristic smell. Highly flammable.

Lye
Any strong alkali used for making soap and for various cleaning operations. Used in many bathroom cleaners and for

unblocking drains. Common household lye is usually sodium hydroxide (caustic soda). It is highly dangerous and can cause severe external as well as internal poisoning. It will burn through cloth, enamel surfaces, brushes, rubber gloves, and damage some metals including aluminum.

Lysol
A very strong and poisonous disinfectant, which is a solution of cresols in soap.

Mineral spirits (paint thinner)
Colorless solvent made from a mixture of mineral oils. Used as a thinner for paints, a general purpose grease and stain remover, and in the manufacture of polish. It helps the polish to spread but evaporates quickly leaving a hard, smooth surface. It is flammable, toxic, and will dry out the natural oils from your hands so use a greasy hand cream after using it. If you wear rubber gloves, wash them afterward. Available in hardware stores.

Moth proofers
Moth proofing products made of paradichlorobenzene are available in block or nugget form to keep moths out of clothes storage cupboards and trunks. Traditional moth balls (also moth flakes) are made of napthalene and smell very strong.

* The green way to deter moths is to put any or all of the following in a muslin bag and place it among the clothes: camphor, lavender, cloves, cinnamon, black pepper, and orris root. Some people also use cedar as a moth repellent.

Muriatic acid
A solution of hydrochloric acid and water, which can be used to clean new bricks and tiles. The solution is dangerous, will damage skin, woodwork, and fabric, and should be used only by professionals.

Naptha

Made from coal tar. Used as a rubber solvent and a solvent for certain greasy stains and in some paints, varnishes and wax polishes. Highly flammable. Don't store at home.

Neat's foot oil

Amber-colored oil from the feet of cows and similar animals. Excellent leather conditioner and protector (but not cleaner). Clean the leather with saddle soap first then rub the oil in with the finger tips. Don't use on shiny surfaces because it is difficult to polish up afterward. From drugstores, shoe shops, hardware shops, and some men's clothing departments.

Neutralizers

Neutralization is something done to remove acid or alkaline residues from clothes after washing. Acetic acid (or white vinegar) will rinse away alkaline residues caused by soap or the deposits left by soap reacting with calcium in hard water, which make colored fabrics look dull. Ammonia rinses remove acidic residues after using sodium hypochlorite bleaches or after using an acid stain remover.

Oven cleaners

The caustic used for cleaning ovens is very strongly alkaline. Wear gloves and don't let it touch any aluminum pans.

Oxalic acid

One of the strongest organic acids. Found in wood sorrel (oxalis) and rhubarb leaves. Highly poisonous. Wear protective gloves. It is used for stain removal and cleaning brassware and also as a bleach and stain remover especially for ink and rust stains. Dissolve ½ teaspoon of oxalic crystals in half a pint of warm water in a glass or china dish. Test before using on nylon or rayon. Rinse well with water.

Paraffins

A group of hydrocarbons obtained from petroleum. Paraffin wax is used in some furniture polishes, in cold creams, and in hair preparations. Liquid paraffins are burned in paraffin stoves and can be useful for removing rust from bicycle and motorcar parts, ancient screws, nuts and bolts, etc. It is poisonous and flammable.

Perchloroethylene
A non-flammable solvent used in most professional dry-cleaning machines.

Petroleum jelly (e.g., Vaseline)
The semi-solid form of mineral oil (distilled from crude oil). Used to lubricate grass stains and other marks, making them easier to remove.

Pumice
Frothy stones of lava from volcanoes. Used for smoothing and cleaning. Powdered pumice is used as an abrasive.

Rottenstone (tripoli)
Used in metal polishes. Mixed with linseed oil it will get rid of white spots on polished wooden furniture. Apply lightly with a soft, clean cloth along the grain of the wood.

Rouge
Jeweler's rouge is a red powder (which also comes in a clay stick) made of ferric oxide. It is used for cleaning and polishing metals, silver, glass, gemstones, etc. Silver polishing cloths are often impregnated with rouge. It is usually available only through a jeweler.

Rust removers and inhibitors
Removers and inhibitors are sometimes incorporated in one product.

- Rust on clothes can be treated with oxalic acid or a commercial dye remover. Slight stains may come out with lemon juice.

- Use steel wool pads to remove rust from kitchen utensils.

- Use a commercial remover from car accessory shops or hardware stores for outdoor tools, bicycles, and cars.

Saddle soap
A special soap used for cleaning leather. Use it on all polished leathers.

Salt (sodium chloride)
Neutral. May be used as an absorbent for liquid stains on carpets. May be used as an absorbent together with olive oil for white ring stains on polished wood furniture.

Silicones
Derived from the mineral silica. They resist water, electricity, weathering, chemicals, and don't react to heat or cold. Used in water-proofed clothing, barrier hand creams, and in small amounts in many polishes, not just for protection but because they help the product to spread. Also included in metal polishes.

Soap
Manufactured from animal fats such as mutton fat, or tallow and olive, or palm-kernel vegetable oils and caustic soda. Builders are often added to household bar soaps and laundry soaps. These include sodium carbonate, borax, water-glass, and sodium phosphates. Don't use such soaps for washing the body.

- A soap is said to be neutral when there is a correct balance between fat and soda. Too much soap will spoil a wash.

Sodium bicarbonate (baking soda)
White powder used as a mild alkali for laundry work. Will remove stains from china, glass, tiles, false teeth, and the refrigerator. You can also wash jewelry in it. Non-poisonous.

Sodium carbonate (washing soda)
Crystalline powder or crystals. Medium alkali for laundry work. Water softener, varnish remover, silver tarnish remover. Useful for cleaning and clearing drains. Do not use on aluminum, silk, wool, sisal, or vinyl flooring. Wear gloves when

using or apply a greasy hand cream after contact. Available in supermarkets.

Sodium hydroxide (sodium hydrate, caustic soda, lye)
A very strong alkali. Used in the manufacture of soap, as a grease remover for ovens, sinks, and drains and as a paint remover. Poisonous and can cause bad skin burns. (See also Caustic soda.)

Sodium perborate
A soft bleach, like Chlorox 2, suitable for all fabrics but don't use a hot solution on heat-sensitive fabrics such as wool, silk, or synthetics.

• When using proprietary sodium perborate preparations follow the manufacturer's directions. Pure sodium perborate crystals can be bought from chemists. Use china or glass and not metal containers to mix the bleach in.

Solvent
A substance used to dissolve another substance. In this book solvent means specifically a liquid that will dissolve the greasy dirt from fabrics. Solvents include perchloroethylene, trichloroethane, and proprietary household spot removers. Denatured alcohol, acetone, amyl acetate, turpentine, isopropyl alcohol, and ether are all solvents. Be careful with these chemicals as they are all flammable and poisonous.

Starch
Usually made from cereals (corn or potato), and used to stiffen fabrics and give them body. Available in powder, liquid, or spray.

Talcum powder
A soft, pliable, greasy, silvery-white powdery mineral. Used as an absorbent.

Teak oil
A treatment for natural teak and other untreated woods; sometimes used instead of polish.

Trichloroethane
A non-flammable and not very toxic solvent used in many proprietary grease stain removers.

Trichloroethylene
Non-flammable solvent used mainly for industrial metal-degreasing applications.

Trisodium phosphate
Similar to washing soda. Sold as TSP in decorating shops for cleaning paint. Use it to clean glazed and unglazed ceramic tiles and most paints. It will make enamel paint dull.

Turpentine
A balsam made from pine trees. Used as a solvent in some paints, varnishes, and waxes. Always use real turpentine when specified as there is no real substitute. Flammable and poisonous.

Vaseline
Trade name for a specific petroleum jelly.

Washing soda
See Sodium carbonate.

Water
Water is the commonest, cheapest cleaner available. It's always worth treating a non-greasy stain with lots of clear water before trying other cleaners. Soft water will produce a lather that lasts 5 minutes when mixed with soap. Hard water doesn't lather easily because of certain salts it has collected when it ran over rocks. Hard water forms a sort of curd with soap, giving a gray look to textiles and damaging the texture. It also appears as a tide line on the bath. Rinsing in water will not get rid of it, but white vinegar can be used to give an acid rinse. Rainwater is soft and good for washing hair and rinsing clothes.

Water softeners
If your water is hard use soapless detergents rather than soap. Washing soda, sodium hexametaphosphate, or sodium sesquicarbonate are all suitable for softening water.

- Plumbed-in water softeners can be fitted into the main water system of a house. Installing such a system is expensive but in areas where the water is very hard it will make washing and cleaning much easier and prevent the furring up of water cisterns and pipes.

Wax
Natural waxes are hard non-greasy solids that do not leave grease marks on paper as other fats do. They are obtained from either plant or animal sources. Waxes are used in various ways for polishing and protecting furniture, cars, shoes, floors, etc. There are also synthetic waxes for use in polishing and waterproofing. Paste waxes are made of wax and mineral spirits. The spirit evaporates leaving a thin film of wax. Liquid waxes are thin creams of wax with an emulsifying agent and water. Silicones may be added to make these polishes spread more easily and help to make them more water-repellent.

- Natural waxes include *carnauba*, which is made from the leaves of a Brazilian palm and is very hard. It is used for furniture, floors, shoes, cars, and toughening other soft waxes and beeswax.

White vinegar
See Acetic acid.

Whiting
Finely ground chalk, free from impurities, used as an abrasive and a coloring in cleaning powder, polishes, and putty.

Index